Knitting Lessons

JEREMY P. TARCHER · PENGUIN
a member of Penguin Group (USA) Inc.
New York

Knitting Lessons

Tales from the Knitting Path

LELA NARGI

Most Tarcher/Penguin books are available at special quantity discounts for bulk purchase for sales promotions, premiums, fund-raising, and educational needs. Special books or book excerpts also can be created to fit specific needs. For details, write Penguin Group (USA) Inc. Special Markets, 375 Hudson Street, New York, NY 10014.

Jeremy P. Tarcher/Penguin
a member of
Penguin Group (USA) Inc.
375 Hudson Street
New York, NY 10014
www.penguin.com

First trade paperback edition 2004
Copyright © 2003 by Lela Nargi

Verses from "Ode to a Pair of Socks" are reprinted from
Odes to Common Things by Pablo Neruda. Copyright © 1994 by Pablo Neruda and Fundación Pablo Neruda (Odes in Spanish); copyright © 1994 by Ken Krabbenhoft (Odes in English); copyright © 1994 by Ferris Cook (illustrations and compilation). Reprinted by permission of Little, Brown and Company, Inc.

The Library of Congress cataloged the hardcover edition as follows:

Nargi, Lela.
Knitting lessons / Lela Nargi.
p.   cm.
Includes bibliographical references.
ISBN 1-58542-210-X
1. Knitting—Patterns.   I. Title.
TT820.N37   2003   2003041014
746.43'2—dc21

ISBN 1-58542-325-4 (paperback edition)

Printed in the United States of America

1   3   5   7   9   10   8   6   4   2

Book design by Claire Vaccaro
Illustrations by Joanna Roy
Sketches of stitches by Lela Nargi

For Rob

&

for Norma

Contents

Knitting Lessons

Introduction

Knitting is creating something where before there was nothing. ("[I]t is on account of emptiness that all things are at all possible, and without emptiness all things will come to naught," said the late-second-century Mahayana dialectician Nagarjuna in his "Discourse on the Middle Path.") Likewise, I would say that my own path toward knitting started with a void rather than any actual stepping stone. This void, creatively speaking, was my grandmother. She didn't knit, but she also didn't crochet or sew; she cooked, but not anything remotely related to nourishment. In my earliest memory of her, she is standing in her fluorescent kitchen, wearing cat's-eye sunglasses, polyester leisure pants, and a pair of blue-and-red Keds; she drags on a Philip Morris unfiltered, picks up a BB gun, shoulders open the screen door, and takes aim at a neighbor's orange-striped tabby, which is innocently, if naïvely, sunbathing in her backyard. Add to this memory vodka, jigsaw puzzles, and coral-colored lipstick, and that basically sums up my grandmother—not exactly what one knitter I met would call a "maker of things" so much as a destroyer of the sanity of house cats.

From this void emerges, rather miraculously, my mother. Where—how, exactly—did my mother learn to paint, draw, sculpt, collage, play the piano, cut out clothing patterns, make buttonholes, cook, embroider, and crochet? As for my mother's knitting, this I can vaguely answer: She learned in a garage-top apartment inhabited by a plump, stern German lady, the hazy image of whom I still hold in an obscure recess of my brain. My path picks up here, only for a moment, but the moment lasts long enough for a short trail to be blazed from one old lady to my mother and finally to me. Because somewhere within this moment some-one—I'm not sure who—handed me yarn and needles and showed me how to knit and how to purl. And this moment, through all the years in which I diligently ignored my mother as she cast off mittens and gloves and brightly striped baby sweaters (her trademark), was sustaining enough to allow me to cling to the overblown idea that one day I would learn to knit again.

"Again" occurred in October 2001, when my path not only picked up but significantly widened. Why hadn't this happened last April? Or October three years ago? If you'd asked me this question at the time, I might have said that my decision to reclaim knitting was random, hap-hazard. Now, looking back, I realize there was nothing especially random about it. For starters, here in Brooklyn, New York, at least, knitting was certainly in the air even before the mainstream media found the dangle of its thread and tugged, and tugged, and tugged. In coffee shops in my neighborhood, on the train, in the park: Suddenly knitters were every-where, where before there had been few—few who were visible, anyway.

Watching these (always) women—young, old, and in-between—I felt an overwhelming desire to join them, to pick up needles and yarn and move my fingers and feel as beneath them fabric emerged. As often as I encountered a single knitter click-clacking away in rapt solitude, I came across two knitters together, or three, knitting and talking, engrossed in their own private universe. And seeing them, I found myself wishing I could whip a wooly swatch from my bag by way of introduction, induction.

I need also to say here, only modestly digressing, that the fact of the month of October 2001 is not insignificant to the equation that leads me back to the path of knitting, or along one of the paths that meanders through this book. All during the months I interviewed knitters, I avoided mentioning September 11. And still it surfaced over and over. Did large numbers of people turn to knitting after this day? Would they never have otherwise? It would be disingenuous of me to speculate. I will say, though, that several people who appear in these pages did decide to learn to knit on the heels of that day. Others admit they returned more rigorously to it, for solace, at a time when we, here in New York especially, were wandering around in a quiet, desperate stupor. In Park Slope, a neighborhood not too far from the two bridges that connect southerly Brooklyn to lower Manhattan, a yarn shop owner and knitting teacher told me that on that day, shell-shocked, soot-covered survivors stumbled off the bridges and into her store, sat down wordlessly on her floor, and began to knit. It seems to me that almost in defiance of the media's insistence that here was a hot new trend, a deeper need for knitting and the comfort it can offer was already, then, very much alive.

So my return to knitting happened in that not-altogether-coincidental month of October 2001, and here, practically speaking, is how: A few blocks from where I live lives a friend of mine from college named Elanor. Elanor is a remarkable knitter—she's a devoted maker of things, generally, but particularly knitted things: beets and other vegetables, handbags, beer bottles reconsidered as penguins, lace scarves, and improvised Irish sweaters. As I'm writing this, Elanor is at work on a life-size human. I visited a few weeks ago to find a nine-pound cone of thick, cream-colored wool hunkering in the middle of her living room, attached by its strand to a full-fledged leg, the pattern for which—toes, knees, ankles, and all—Elanor had conceived by gazing back and forth between her needles and her own leg. One day in October, another mutual friend asked Elanor if she'd teach her how to knit. Stricken with a strange fear of finding myself somehow left behind, I said, "Teach me, too." Of course, she did. For all matters related to knitting, she's been my touchstone ever since.

As I embarked upon the adventure of learning (or relearning) how to knit, one question kept surfacing in my mind: *Why? Why do I find myself so inexplicably drawn to knitting? Why do so many others?* In writing this book, I hoped to at least begin to answer that question.

Why knit? Some of the reasons I discovered as I interviewed knitters across the country weren't all that surprising, given the underlying nature of knitters: They had to do with highly personal, though often articulated, ideas regarding generosity, and spirituality, and consumerism, and feminism, and the interconnectedness of life and art. Some of the answers were greatly surprising, and those answers are tucked in among these pages, waiting to be given new life in the reading.

Most of all, though, this book marks a path. Like Matsuo Bashō, the seventeenth-century Japanese haiku master and student of Zen who re-

4

corded his experiences as a traveler—the people he met, the landscapes he cherished—in such books as *The Narrow Road to the Deep North* and *The Records of a Weather-Exposed Skeleton,* I set out to travel through the varied landscape of knitting. As I've mentioned, my path had been narrowly forged before, linking me to an admittedly shallow knitting heritage that began only with my mother. Not knowing where the path would lead, this past spring I began to follow it from individual knitters to yarn shops, to Internet sites, to crafting groups, to magazines, to old knitting books—evidence of a heritage vast enough to sustain any knitter—in New York and the Midwest and California and back east to Maine. Herein is recorded that path, which now links my past to my present, my life as a knitter to the lives of other knitters, and a divergent group of knitters each to the other, on a small scale creating what I discovered along the way to be perhaps the greatest of knitting's achievements: creating community.

Knitting Lessons

It can happen to you. In a flashing moment something opens. You are new all through. You see the unsame world with fresh eyes.

—Ekai, *The Gateless Gate*

I want to make socks." This I announced to my friend Elanor on the evening of our first knitting lesson. A sweater seemed too great a commitment, an afghan hopelessly humdrum. Scarves, dishcloths, hats:

everyone's first project. I wanted something with a little more pizzazz. I'm sure I had a notion that socks were, and would be for a while, beyond my ken. I'm sure I realized that the kind of socks I was picturing—conjured not from any grounding in practicality on my part, or with even a vague nod to reason, but rather encouraged to blossom to near-mythic intricacy in the overfertile recesses of my imagination—were more complicated than I would admit. And I'm sure that somewhere in the back of my mind I knew that I would never have the patience to puzzle out knee-highs patterned with markings like the ones you find on old silk stockings—a narrow black line running up the calf; a trapezoid, a half-moon cradling the heel and the toe—knitted tightly, on tiny needles, with something silky and thin.

Elanor, determined to be supportive: "*Hmm,* yes, socks," she said, blinking away from my ridiculously stubborn expression to contemplate the gloss of red paint coating her living room wall. "Socks are a great project. But maybe not a *first* project." I grimaced, probably, pretending to smile in deference to Elanor's vast knitting experience, but really I was thinking, *Socks . . . I will make socks.*

I didn't make socks. Sipping tea from an old English teacup as I sat with my feet planted flat on Elanor's couch, I made a bizarrely satisfying ball from a skein of rainbow-colored yarn I'd chosen several days before at a local knitting shop, unwinding it from its orbit around my knees. I let Elanor cast on for me and show me how to make a knit stitch. And then I made a cramped, lopsided row of purple and red, and another. Then, for a row of red and pink, the yarn I had wrapped around my left forefinger for tension suddenly began to glide instead of catch as I knit.

Each stitch, then each row, picked up its own rhythm—a silent one; looping wool around bamboo needles is not a noisy undertaking—that matched my breathing. My tea grew cold in its cup as row after row fell away, a narrow strip of cloth gathering bulk between my palms. Somewhere in the midst of all this, Elanor exclaimed, "Hey, look, you knit continental!" a revelation that for the moment meant nothing to me. But several days later, I happened upon two young women in a local café who were knitting American-style, grasping their yarn in a manner that looked backward to me, and I understood that for better or worse, without even trying, I knit like my mother. And in an instant, knitting seemed oddly *right,* fraught as it was with history and heredity.

I think I had an inkling of the connection that very first night, too, when I went home from Elanor's to work the skein in my own living room. I pushed myself ever so slightly back and forth in my rocking chair while my needles worked feverishly through the yarn. My face felt tight; I'd unconsciously pulled it into a half-smile, half-contortion of concentration. My husband looked up from his book and asked me a question, which I answered with a mindless *"Mmmmmm,"* meant to indicate that I had heard his question and was processing it; really, though, I hadn't heard a word he'd said. This was familiar behavior—motherlike behavior—but not behavior that had ever been my own . . . until now.

I finished the skein that night—determined to finish it, like a person possessed. I left it still fastened to its needle when I went to bed—a narrow, foreshortened strip of alternating color only slightly less useless than a three-fingered glove. Still, I was delighted with it; it was soft and pleasingly textured, and free of holes or knots or any other unbargainedfor anomalies. The next morning, sheepish about calling Elanor—she'd retaught me how to knit; could I really expect her to teach me everything else?—I found a knitting how-to site online and taught myself how to cast off. Then I taught myself how to cast on, in an inexplicable panic to start—or, I'll be honest, finish—another skein, this time of soft blue-green yarn. I knit a few rows, managed to create a pattern of bizarre, ladder-backed holes by misconstruing some directions for increasing that my friend Lydia read to me over the phone from a "learn to knit and crochet" pamphlet she'd once bought at a thrift store, then cast off a small rectangle that was . . . unique. Elanor phoned, wondering why I hadn't called her to ask about casting off, and the next morning I was back at her house, practicing purling at her kitchen table.

Then Elanor said, "I think you're ready to see something." She got up from the table and came back to it carrying an innocuous, lavender-colored paperback. She handed it over. "It" was *Mary Thomas's Book of Knitting Patterns*. I flipped through pages peppered with line-drawn motifs of stockinette, and seed stitch, and checks, and basket-weave. *That's all very nice*, I thought, as I contemplated the images and their accompanying instructions. Then: a split second of revelation, and my brain froze. I looked up at Elanor and spluttered, "Do you mean to tell me that there are only *two stitches?*" She silently beamed back at me, like a kindergarten teacher who means to show you how delighted she is that you have managed, for the first time, to color inside the lines. At that moment, nubs and ribbings, loops and stripes, a whole universe of knitting once-mysteries resounded in my mind as a giant answer.

Back at home again, I made another rectangle, alternating knits and purls and holes, and then another, and another, until the blue-green yarn was all finished up. Then, like an imbecile, inordinately and ridiculously proud of myself, I stitched the patches of yarn together to fashion a cover for an ugly pillow that had been taking up space in my closet for years.

Somewhere along the line I had forgotten all about socks.

1.

Williamsburg Diary

For months before I began work on this book, I encountered knitters everywhere. Naturally, the minute I set out to find them they became weirdly scarce. Jessica, a woman who lives in my Williamsburg, Brooklyn, neighborhood, and who I used to see nearly every morning in the park and occasionally sitting on the subway with her latest sweater creation evolving under her hands and onto her lap, virtually disappeared. My favorite café became emptied of winter's gaggle of knitters. I left messages for knitting friends-of-friends and came to expect that my calls would go unanswered. This was not an auspicious beginning. But it was spring, after all, a season when some of the most afflicted of knitters have been known to set aside their needles, even if it's only for a week or two, because they are accustomed to knitting with wool, and that material feels suddenly too thick and hot for the climate, or because the newfound lightness of the April air seems to give license to a few moments of unaccustomed inactivity.

The first knitter I found, sometime in May, was a photographer named Erika deVries. I found her through a mutual friend who manages a gift shop in my neighborhood that sells sweaters and skirts made of cotton or merino by a group of expert expatriate Nepali women. Erika goes to the shop often—as does pretty much everyone in the neighborhood, myself included—to ogle the handknits. "I was always falling in love with those sweaters, but they were out of my price range," Erika told me. "And I thought, *I could make those!*"

One bright morning, I walked over to meet Erika at her studio, a high-ceilinged, windowless room hung with her collages and photos. The baseboards of the room were lined with flat files and magazines and Erika's napping dog, Birdie; the floor was stacked with papers and shopping bags crammed with months worth of her knitting projects, fashioned from thickly textured and colorful yarns: several monochromatic scarves, a triangular mohair shawl, one variegated turtleneck sweater, and a new project of large, lilac-and-orange swatches, on which she was practicing color changes and patterns. As Erika talked, one by one she pulled her projects out from the shopping bags until they covered every near surface.

Erika deVries

*Everyone has a friend who, in a few
minutes will teach them the first steps
of this fascinating occupation.*

—Jane Eyre, *Needles and Brushes*
and How to Use Them, 1887

I had back surgery on October 11—pretty simple surgery for a disk,
but if you've never had surgery before it's a little overwhelming. My
friend Joseph is a gifted maker of things, and I asked him to teach me
how to knit. Joseph sat on my bed, and we knit and we talked about our
families. I live deep in Brooklyn, and people don't really come over very
much, so it was nice to have some attention. He was really good at teaching me, which in my previous experiences had not been the case—a
friend had tried to teach me on a road trip, but I was just too much of a
spaz to learn; and my mother had tried to get me to knit in high school
with a woman who taught, but I was much more interested in watching
her teenage sons. In October, I was just ready to focus on something new.

The first thing I knit was a black square. We had an art show at New
York University, where I teach, of responses to September 11; all the
work had to be 8" x 8". I couldn't even think about picking up my camera
at that point; it seemed like a really obscene object. I had just been sitting
at home learning to knit with Joseph—that was a beautiful thing about my
back surgery, that Joseph came over and we spent all this time together—
and knitting seemed like the right thing to do. I knit a black square in

stockinette stitch. It was internal, and it was the only thing I could think of. I got the yarn at the Union Square farmer's market, from a woman who sells sheepskins and her own spun wool. I didn't realize you were supposed to roll the skein into a ball, and it became this big mess. And I didn't know how to stop; I didn't know how to stop knitting. I walked into The Yarn Tree in Williamsburg, Brooklyn, with this big, old hairy mass, and Linda, the owner, was so nice. She said, "OK, you should wind this first. . . ." And as I was leaving, after she'd helped me cast off, she said, "You know, we teach classes." And I've been taking classes there ever since.

Linda and I just collaborated on a sweater. [Erika holds up a red, yellow, and blue variegated turtleneck.] I did all the knitting, but she got me there. If I weren't working with Linda, or if Joseph had just taught me and then disappeared, I probably would have stopped knitting, because I really need someone around I can talk to and ask questions of. I like being in a class, being out of the house, and knitting with my friends on Sunday nights. That really keeps me grounded in a project. Everyone in the city is always working so hard that they don't have time to connect with other people in more meaningful and longer ways than having coffee. Being an artist, I don't have a workplace where people are happy to see me, so Linda's shop is a nice place to go; it punctuates my week. I also love the solitude of knitting, but I feel as though I need a place to check in, to say, "Here's what I'm doing." Unless you're Henry Darger,* you're making things to share them, ultimately.

With this sweater, I had to take one of the sleeves out. That was frus-

*A reclusive Chicago janitor and "Outsider Artist" who spent some forty years writing and illustrating his novel, *The Realms of the Unreal,* and other works, which were only found after his death in 1973.

trating, but it was good—I have to learn how to let go; that's one of the best lessons in knitting. Joseph told me that he'd knit an entire sweater, but he didn't like the way it looked, so he took it all out and did it again. That left such a huge impression on me. Taking something out bothers me, but I get over it pretty fast. This shell [she fishes out a simple, sleeveless garment] originally wasn't wide enough; Linda held onto it while I pulled it out and I wound it into a ball. Ten hours of knitting gone in three minutes. But now I know that it'll happen again in a matter of hours. The idea of letting go has been really good for me, and I've been able to let that spill over into letting go of feeling upset about other things.

What I love about knitting is that it's this thing that becomes another thing, and I really like the repetition involved in it. It's kind of like sewing, but more long-term; you can do it for hours without having to get up and cut something. It's also been good for my art. I come from California, and I used to love to drive great distances; there's something about the feeling of space that sparks creative thinking. Knitting does that, too.

In the last week and a half, I haven't wanted to knit at all. I feel like I'm at a point where I'm ready for a transition, and I'm a little freaked out by the idea of it. When I first started, I just felt like I was learning all the time. I'm still learning, but now I have a lot more skills, and the knitting needs to come together in another way. I'm working on a mural project with my photographs, and I think I will knit something for it— whenever I'm making any kind of art, I always try to incorporate everything that's informing the moment. I'll probably just knit some big blotch, and I'll collage it.* Maybe that's all I'll ever do with it. But I do feel like the knitting needs to become something else now. I know my other art so well. A couple weeks ago, the f-stops weren't moving on my camera, but I didn't realize it, so all these rolls of film I shot were totally overexposed. Originally, I thought I'd done something wrong, and for two days I was so mad at myself until I sat with my camera and played with everything and realized the camera is actually busted. Until I figured that out, I felt like, "I've been doing this for twelve years; I should know better." With knitting, I don't feel that way—I'm a beginner. And you can't really ruin yarn. You just start over.

A story I remember from when I was a kid: My dad was an airline pilot and he brought me this purse from Japan that was shaped like a panda bear head. I carried it everywhere. One day, my mom took me to the fabric store, and when we came home, I went into her room and said, "Look what I got at the fabric store, Mommy." I dumped my purse out and it was full of thread—I had pulled all the colors I liked out of the thread bin and put them in my purse. I feel like that when I'm in the yarn store—I want to put the yarn all around me. My yarn bag is clear, so I can see all the skeins.

Until a week and a half ago, I would stay up knitting until I was falling over on the couch. I couldn't stop. I would say to myself, *Oh, just two more rows and I can go to sleep.* I like it so much that it's hard to stop. Or I put it aside and do other things and then say, *OK, after I do these*

---

*That's precisely what she did, for a show that ran in a gallery in Manhattan in July—Erika took the orange-and-lavender swatches she'd been knitting when we met and hung them commingled with her pictures.

things, then I can let myself knit. It's becomes that thing for me, the thing that I would prefer to be doing. I feel like I'm hooked, like a drug.

From Erika, I progressed naturally on to her teacher, Linda, who last year, on a whim, opened her yarn shop—The Yarn Tree—in the largely Hispanic section of my neighborhood. The shop became an instant hub: a place for locals to meet, talk, commiserate, and most of all, of course, share their knitting.

I'd met Linda before, when I'd gone into her shop to buy yarn and needles for my first knitting lesson at Elanor's house. It was a cold autumn evening, dark already at 6 P.M. The shop was warmly lit and empty except for Linda and her dog, Barley, who was curled up in a snug C amid yarn baskets clustered on the windowsill. Linda appeared for a minute to give me a loud hello (Barley barely lifted her head) and then, sensing perhaps that I wanted to be left alone to browse, disappeared again into the back room, where she keeps her weaving studio. I walked from shelf to shelf, letting my fingers drift along the mounds of yarn, mesmerized.

"I don't want to sell the same yarns every other yarn store is selling," Linda would later say to me. And she certainly doesn't—most of her yarns come from small companies on the East Coast. Right off the bat, even to someone who knows nothing about yarn (certainly me on that night of my first visit), the difference is palpable. The yarns come in unusual colors—some muted and vaguely "off," like a flat note on a piano; some strikingly vibrant and true—and inconsistent textures. The look of

them is unspeakably alluring. That first night, gazing at the yarn as behind me, from the night, entered a stream of Linda's devotees charged
up for class, I could not choose from among them: cottony Colinette
yarns, in variegations of pale green and pink, or pumpkin orange and
gray; a triple-plied twist of superfine alpaca in beige and burnt umber
and sienna; rougher "Mountain Mohair," with color names straight out
of a J. Crew catalog: Edelweiss and Balsam and Day Lily; a laceweight,
grape-hued blend made from the fur of possums; wool dyed by Linda
herself, including a particularly vivid shade she calls "Statue of Liberty
Green." How *could* a person be expected to choose?

At the back table, the gathered women began unpacking their knitting gear, talking and cackling and greeting a reemerged Linda, who was
now flitting happily among them, visibly pleased to be surrounded by
people who needed her. She brought with her an enormous box—a new
shipment of another item that makes her shop so unusual: Brillo-like
batts from the karakul, or fat-tailed sheep, sent up from a farm in Cul-
peper, Virginia, which would be used by one of her classes to make felt.
At the sight of the batts, an astonished exclamation emanated from the
knitters. I felt suddenly conspicuous in my ignorance and indecision and
solitude, and wished I had some pertinent question or comment to offer.

I let myself be drawn back over to a shelf of vegetable-dyed, hand-
plied merino/angora yarns from Jamie Harmon in Vermont: soft and
luscious, with colors derived from cochineal—a dye made from the dried
bodies of a certain Southern insect—and Osage oranges and onion skins
and indigo and madder root. With considerable effort, I narrowed my
desire to two skeins—those yarns on which I'd later conduct my first awkward knitting experiments: one single-strand skein of a light, rich green

whose tint was a cross between sage and sea-foam, flecked here and there with hints of cream or yellow or sky; and one double-plied skein—that same misty blue-green twined with pink, then purple, then yellow, then giving way to sky blue, then red, and so on. As I approached the register, a woman at the back table held up a hat she'd just completed that morning. "Oh, that's beautiful!" cried Linda, and a cheer went up in the room. I paid for my yarn and walked back out into the night, wishing I'd had the courage to make that little community of women, so noisily busy and enthusiastic there in Linda's cheerful yarn shop, somehow my own.

LINDA LaBELLE

Let him first find what is right and then he can teach it to others.
—*THE DHAMMAPADA*

I was going to make this space into a crafts gallery to support my looms, because I'm primarily a weaver and a costume designer. I wasn't feeling great about opening the gallery, though—it didn't seem to fit in with the neighborhood. At the time, I was working on a film with the artist Matthew Barney, *Cremaster 3*. For one of the scenes we were shooting, I'd taught the principal how to spin, and I'd taught her how to do a five-finger walking braid, and I brought out yarns for her to manipulate on-screen. When she took a break off-camera, I was handling the yarns, and there was a lot of static electricity in them. I called for

Kim, my assistant, to cut me some fresh yarn. There was someone observing over Matthew's shoulder, and he got this funny look on his face, because I guess what I said sounded funny. So Kim brought me fresh yarn, and we got the shot in one take and the guy said to Matthew, "Wow, Linda really knows her yarn." And Matthew said, really strongly, "Linda *does* know her yarn." I went home that night and had trouble sleeping. I kept running that over and over in my head. I woke up the next morning and said, "Son of a bitch, I *do* know my yarn," and that day I did the paperwork to open this shop. I didn't do a business plan, I didn't think it through. I just knew I wanted to teach because I love doing it, and I love fiber and color, and yarn is something I know a lot about.

I'm a designer, and that's the way I teach—I try to make things work for people. I believe all of us can be our own designers, given the tools. We can figure out how to make something, we can make it happen. That's the excitement. I teach professional techniques so people can make the simplest things and make them look beautiful. I've always taught something—horseback riding and skiing. Knitting is more personal, especially since this is my personal space, my studio. Believe it or not, I'm incredibly solitary. For me to open this up to people every day is quite different; if I weren't enjoying it, I'd close the doors. Kim and I worked for two years on a project, during which we never saw anybody. Now, maybe sixty people come in for classes a week.

I didn't know what to expect when I opened The Yarn Tree, but what's happened is that the shop has created a community. In this neighborhood, there are very few places people can gather other than a bar. Here there's no pretense, and everyone is so supportive: "Oh, let me see what you're doing!" and "That's fantastic!" The other night, one woman finished a sock and another woman finished her sweater, and we were all hugging and kissing and clapping, and there was someone else here, and she was so close to finishing the sweater she was working on that we wouldn't let her leave. It got later and later and later, but we said, "We're going to get you through it." And we did. There's a small-town atmosphere here, and I love it.

 The Yarn Tree's Monday-night class consists of three women, all in their thirties, all from completely divergent backgrounds: Mary Elizabeth Walker is a mild-tempered African-American musician originally from Lawrence, Kansas; Mitzi Good is a hip-looking, wisecracking art director; and Dinna Díaz, who grew up in East New York, Brooklyn, is a Hispanic stay-at-home mom and freelance makeup artist. When I met the group, they'd been together for nine months and four classes, and had no intention of giving each other up anytime soon.

What struck me most about the women on the night I met them in the shop (a visit that coincided nicely with my desire to fondle Linda's yarns) was that they talked nonstop as they knit. My presence didn't slow them down a bit. And listening to them with my eyes closed for a few seconds every now and then, I realized it would be easy to mistake them for siblings, or at least the best of friends.

The Yarn Tree's Monday-Night Class

In the "good old times" of our grandmothers, every young girl was taught to knit as she was taught to read—it was a necessary part of her education. But in these days, looms and knitting machines have crowded hand labor almost entirely out of the market, and the elegant art of hand knitting has fallen almost entirely into disuse. Many young ladies have never learned to make even the simplest articles but must depend on stores for everything they need.

—The Self-Instructor in Silk Knitting,
Crochet and Embroidery, 1884

MARY WALKER: I saw Linda's ad in the paper and I thought, *Wow, a knitting store in the neighborhood.* So I stopped by and got the information on classes, but I hadn't committed to one. Then September 11 happened and I got so stressed out; I couldn't turn off the TV; I couldn't sleep at night. I was talking to my mom, and I told her about the knitting class and she said, "Sign up for it, sign up for it and *do it.*" I think I was just driving her crazy. So I took the class and it did take my mind off all those other things.

DINNA DÍAZ: September 15 was our first class. We took beginning knitting. Then we did a sweater, mittens, socks . . .

MITZI GOOD: . . . puppets.

DINNA: Mitzi did a puppet, because she only did one sock.

MITZI: I turned it into a puppet!

DINNA: The three of us took spinning together. We've dyed yarn. Linda lets us do whatever we want. We decide we're going to do a project, and then we just do it. I have a little one, and that's what made me want to start knitting, when I was pregnant. I said, "I'm going to teach myself how to knit so that I can knit things for the baby." I bought a bunch of knitting stuff, and I would sit there at night watching television, trying to teach myself how to knit. Then my husband said, "They opened a knitting shop on Bedford Avenue. You should check it out—it's right up your alley." It's really hard to learn from a book; I'm much better one-on-one or with a teacher. I understand by watching people.

MITZI: I started knitting a scarf on my own about this time last year. I was going to make it for my sister's birthday. I started this one yesterday. [She holds up an almost-complete olive-green mohair scarf in loose garter stitch.] The other one I worked on for months and months. I thought maybe I remembered how to knit from when I was a child. Then I saw that there was a yarn store in the neighborhood, so I came in to check it out and spontaneously signed up for knitting lessons, realizing that my scarf was not really how it should have been.

LINDA LABELLE: Tell the story!

MITZI: I glued the yarn together.

DINNA: She glued the yarn together! [Shrieks of laughter fill the room.]

MITZI: I didn't know how to change colors, so I tied a knot then cut it as close to the knot as possible, and then eventually the knot would get loose and I'd have these two ends, and that's when I got the glue out. [laughter] Linda was very polite.

LINDA: I laughed!

MITZI: No, not the first time I came in. She was polite, and now that I know Linda and her quality of knitting, she probably burst out laughing the second I left.

LINDA: I said, "If I were to knit this scarf, I wouldn't do it this way. . . ."

MITZI: Knitting is just something really nice you can do at night, just sit and not have to think too hard. My husband likes to watch TV, and I don't always get into the storyline as deeply as he does. So it's a way to spend time together, but not. [laughter] When we started, I thought that making a sweater was going to be the ultimate, which is what we did in the second class. Now I like having big projects, little projects, everything. I'm just over the top. I also like the fact that the three of us are totally multi-culti gal pals. I don't think our circles ever would've crossed if it weren't for this class.

DINNA: We've even hung out outside of class. They helped me paint my new apartment.

LINDA: Dinna called from Puerto Rico to say hello to the class.

DINNA: I was on vacation and I thought, *They're knitting today!* I really enjoy coming here, and when I don't get to, I miss it.

LINDA: Dinna taught a class here—bikini-making.

DINNA: Mitzi was a whiz at spinning. We took the class with her. [to Mary] Didn't she pick it up *like that?* She was better than the teacher. So we told Linda to get rid of that teacher and put Mitzi in there. Now Mitzi teaches spinning here.

MITZI: I think it's a hand-eye coordination thing. I used to twirl batons. [laughter] It's trusting what's going on down here while you're working up here. It's the same thing as baton twirling: You throw it up in the air, and then you trust that it's going to be right in front of you when you're ready. As soon as you feel that energy and that pull, and you know you've made this little piece of yarn, it's addictive. And if you're knitting, it's so satisfying to know that you've taken this fleece and turned it into something beautiful.

MARY: I've seen movies with big giant spinning wheels and people spinning, and I wanted to learn how to do that. It's just neat to make your own things. How many people can spin fleece into yarn, dye it, and make something from it? It's powerful.

DINNA: I love being able to start from scratch. I sew as well—I like taking fabric and cutting out a pattern; there's a satisfaction you get from being able to say, "I made this." People ask, "Why didn't you just go to the store and buy it?" Because it doesn't mean the same thing. It makes me feel good that I took a lot of time to make something. When you go shopping for something, you can never quite find what you want.

MITZI: So you get it in black. For each class, we agree that we want to do some particular project, and then we talk about it. Everyone agrees to it.

DINNA: In the last class, we decided we would do socks and mittens, but I wasn't here the day that they decided *which* socks to make. We ended up doing a petite lace rib pattern from the Koigu sock book. Every class, I was cursing, "Who picked this damn pattern?" But I loved the mittens—I made three pairs.

MITZI: I made three pairs, too—gave them away, and I'm regretting it every second. They're for sale; now they cost $500. [laughter] I'm all about giving!

MARY: I started wanting to knit because I was spending so much money on hats.

DINNA: Every week she would come in here with a new hat and we'd say, "*Oooh*, that's a nice hat. How much did you pay for that?"

LINDA: She has a great head for hats.

MITZI: You could put a paper bag on her head and it would look great.

MARY: For the first class, I made quite a few.

DINNA: I sew, but when I made my first hat, I couldn't figure out how to sew it together.

LINDA: And remember the pizza. . . .

DINNA: I washed the hat and I thought, *Oh this is so cool,* and I was spinning it on my finger and Linda said, "You're stretching it out." I was spinning it like pizza dough.

Another reason I like to come here is that my daughter commands a lot of my attention—she's sixteen months old now. Even when my husband takes her to another room, I can hear her crying. If I can get out of the house and go somewhere, it's easier to concentrate.

LINDA: And plus there are other people.

MITZI: There's a social aspect. You can see projects that other people are doing, like that girl, Rachel, with the gloves. I say, "I want to use *that* color."

MARY: It's a creative environment. People are here because they want to be here. That makes it great. I also think introspective, doing-it-alone-at-home knitting is wonderful, because it gives you an option. You feel like you're doing something positive.

MITZI: When I lost my job last fall, I treated knitting like a job; I'd knit, knit, knit. It was like a sweatshop in my house. I couldn't just relax and kick back and do nothing.

DINNA: When I'm knitting at home alone, it's my time. Or if I want to knit in front of the television, it's still my time. I feel guilty if I sit around doing nothing. I even brought knitting on my vacation to Puerto Rico.

MARY: I go to visit a friend who lives out in Queens, and every time I go to see her that's forty-five minutes on the train. So I knit. People are always staring at me.

DINNA: The first time I took out my knitting needles on the train, it was weird to have everybody looking at me. Then the second or third time I did it I was like, "I don't care, I have an *hour.*" I've seen other people knitting, but I haven't gone up to them—I guess maybe because when I'm knitting I'm in the zone, and I'm respecting that person's space.

MITZI: I put out bad vibes: "Go away!"

LINDA: Some students say they've been approached on the train, because I teach American knitting and people who knit continental will tell them they're doing it wrong. One girl had this woman grab her sweater out of her hand and start knitting.

MITZI: That's when the needle becomes a weapon.

DINNA: Mary, I found something for you. I went to another knitting store. I was scoping it out for you, Linda—totally scoping it out! The yarns were not as nice as this, but they did have a lot of magazines and pattern books, and I bought some for Miss Mary. They had two patterns for skirts.

MARY: I've been wanting to make a skirt for a long time, an A-line skirt, but I haven't seen any patterns. I guess knitted skirts are done with machines these days.

LINDA: We're approaching making our own patterns now. We've done it in baby steps, a little bit at a time. Right now, they're making a sweater from *Rebecca* magazine, and they're rewriting the pattern to make it simpler to knit and to fit each body type.

DINNA: We're going to make it without the turtleneck.

MARY: I think it'll be more versatile without the turtleneck.

DINNA: We try to find things that are doable, that we can figure out. Still, I always feel as though I need a pattern to work from so I can see what the finished product looks like. It takes such an investment of my time to make it that to design it on my own, if I don't know what it's going to look like . . . I don't think I'm there yet.

MITZI: That was the weird thing with that cardigan; I didn't know what it would look like.

LINDA: They made a body, then chose everything as they went along: the cuffs and the collar and the ribbing.

DINNA: Mine had three different colors.

MITZI: Mary's had crochet on the edges that Dinna did for her, and bell sleeves; mine looked like a bowling jacket.

DINNA: I couldn't deal with working on such small needles, so I picked a thicker yarn.

MARY: I love this cold summer—I wore my sweater last week. People don't notice that I made it; they say, "I really like your sweater," and then I say, "Thanks, I made it."

MITZI: Then they analyze it and say, "Oh, that's so cool."

MARY: I'm more picky about the quality of all my clothing in general now. If I go into a store and a top is $80, it has to justify itself to me. If it isn't sewn right, then I won't buy it. Now I also realize why some things are so expensive. I've learned so much from Linda about fibers and textiles.

MITZI: This is more than a yarn shop. Linda's got her studio here, and whole sheep fleeces come in. Where have you ever seen a whole sheep fleece before?

So Begins a Fetish

The cloth exists on account of the thread.

—Pingalaka

I stumbled upon the beginnings of a yarn sale one morning when I'd rolled out of bed and onto the street to buy a loaf of bread for breakfast. I stood on the corner, rubbing my eyes in disbelief, as boxes and boxes and boxes of yarn were hauled out of a neighborhood shop (the same gift shop that carries its own line of handknits) and unceremoniously plunked onto the concrete. It was only 9 A.M. on a Saturday, and there weren't many other people out and about yet; I was the very first, and very lucky, patron of the day. As I stepped up to the little wool outpost, my heart began to race with anticipation.

Funny—*strange*—how quickly other people materialized on the so recently deserted streets, as though some psychic channel for all yarn junkies within a five-mile radius had somehow yawned open. As I pawed through the boxes, I could feel a small crowd gathering behind me. Several members of the assembly approached and began to rummage alongside me. I picked up my pace, catching my breath, gritting my teeth, and grabbing for anything that looked, in my mounting concern that someone would beat me to *the best* ball of wool, even marginally soft or colorful. I tucked potential worthies into my armpits, then under my chin, then into the waistband of my pants. I dug and dug, every once in a while casting a quick glance upward to see what goodies were currently being carted out of the shop (large cones, then sweater remnants), and to monitor the actions of my fellow shoppers.

With balls of yarn looped, finally, onto my fingers and no place else to hold them, I waddled up to the checkout table. Just in time. The yarn, not to be contained a moment longer, exploded off my body in every direction. The woman behind the register collected the balls into a neat pile and gave me a dubious look. I smiled back at her, trying to show her that I was respectable. I discovered a stray ball of wool down my shirt, plucked it out, and lay it demurely on the table. The woman tallied up my haul—$70. Was that all? I opened my wallet and discovered that I had no money.

More and more yarn shoppers were assembling, and I could see a few of them eyeing my stash. "Don't worry," said the woman. "I'll watch it for you until you get back." I thanked her, but didn't quite trust her promise. As fast as I could, I ran for Pedro's Grocery, the nearest shop with an ATM. Closed. I ran another block to the Mini Mall, where the ATM happened to be broken. Panicked and out of breath, I dragged myself three blocks back in the opposite direction to Superior Market and finally—*finally*—dispensed myself a wad of crisp twenties. Exhausted now, I plodded back to the yarn sale. As I trudged, I began to ask myself, "Can I really afford to spend $70 on mismatched balls of yarn? Will I ever really use half a skein of lime-and-white wool? And if so, for *what?*" Thus it happened that I was a calmer, more reasonable woman by the time I returned to the checkout table. I picked slowly through my pile, weeding. Each ball of wool I set to the side was snatched in a flash by one of a circling brood of yarn vultures.

At last, I settled on a $10 bag of caramel-colored blended wool; a ball of nubby, chocolatey merino; and another ball of merino, in butter yellow. My purchases packed neatly into a shopping bag, and twelve new dollars handed happily over for their exchange, I did feel almost respectable as I ambled casually back home—breakfast and bread be damned—leaving a seething, frenzied mob in my wake.

2 .

Records of an Invisible Trail:
"Talking" to Knitters I've
Never Met

After I'd interviewed Erika, and Linda and her students, I had a difficult time all over again in finding knitters. My phone calls to various "leads" led nowhere, and the coffee shops continued to yield up not
a single yarn-carrying craftsperson. As I was becoming truly desperate, I
attempted to explain to a Korean woman who was picking through yarn
remnants outside the handknit shop—this was late in the afternoon,
when I just "happened" to be passing by again, long after I'd brought my
own stash home—that I was writing a book and wanted to interview
people about knitting. "I'm not interested," she said, irritated and blinking fast behind her glasses. No doubt she suspected that I was attempting to distract her from the yarn for my own nefarious purposes. Or
maybe she—maybe everyone I'd tried to contact—was convinced, like
camera-shy tribes who refuse to be photographed, that by talking to me

about her knitting she would somehow be offering up an irretrievable bit of her soul.

Not knowing where else to turn, I began looking for knitters on the Internet. This idea had seemed preposterous to me at the very outset of my project—I think the combination of the ancient, mannered craftiness of knitting and the techie anonymity of computers struck me as essentially incongruous. But the Internet proved to be a great resource on more than one occasion. Online, I found instructions for casting off and making lace; knitting with beads; stranding and dying; tips on buying needles; reviews of yarn, books, and shops; profiles of famous knitters and knitwear designers; links to everything knitting-related under the sun. Surfing around, I also happened to find *Knitter's Review*, an online magazine whose forum hosts some 10,000 knitters from all across the country. I lurked there for a while, sheepishly, until I found a few posts whose authors struck me as engaging and pleasantly opinionated. The first of them was written by Elizabeth Morse, who identified herself as experiencing a "minor identity crisis" from her decision to knit. "There is," she said, "some guilt in rediscovering the hobbies of my grandmother, since they harken back to an age . . . from which my mother worked so hard to escape. I feel slightly rebellious doing it." Elizabeth's post intrigued me; we are roughly the same age, and the influence of feminism on her decision to knit (or not to), took me by surprise, if only because it was so far removed from my own experience.

I contacted Elizabeth, fully expecting her to accuse me of web-based voyeurism and refuse to speak with me. Instead, she wrote me a long letter from the boarding school in Montezuma, New Mexico—the

United World College of the American West—where she teaches English to non-native speakers and also runs a popular evening knitting activity.

Elizabeth Morse

As a creative outlet or soother of nerves, [knitting] is unexcelled, providing you with an easy, relaxing pursuit you can pick up, take with you, or leave off at will.

—Isabelle Stevenson,

The Big Book of Knitting, 1948

I learned to knit only three summers ago, in the summer of 1999, when I was twenty-eight years old. I had always wanted to learn to knit and had attempted it as a teenager. I remember going into the tiny, dusty yarn shop in my hometown of Gaylord, Michigan, which was run by the grandmother of someone I knew at school. The shop was so small that you could not invisibly browse; upon entering, a quite frightening old lady confronted me, and when I said I wished to learn to knit, she sat me down to teach me then and there. As soon as she saw that I was left-handed, however, her manner became even more gruff. She insisted on teaching me to knit right-handed, in what I now know is the continental style. I went back to her a few times and then stopped. It wasn't fun, and I didn't really understand the process. I may not have even gotten beyond casting on.

In college, the living room of my dormitory was beautiful, with a working fireplace and a piano and a window seat overlooking the courtyard. I often watched with some envy as my housemates knitted and chatted in that gorgeous space. But I did not ask to be taught. I was far out of my social realm in that rare, collegial environment, and perhaps I didn't want to embark on a project at which I could fail. More likely, I think, I disdained what I saw as a "leisure activity"; surely my time would be better spent honing my mind than chatting and playing with string.

I lived in Japan when I was in my early twenties. I knew that taking up some craft would be a good idea; I needed something to fill the many hours of loneliness one experiences when living alone abroad. However, the materials required for knitting were too expensive for me, and the thought of trying to learn from scratch via written or oral Japanese was too much. I learned origami instead—paper was cheap, and children loved to show me how to make things. Then, when I was in graduate school, I needed a nonacademic pursuit to keep me balanced, but I failed to engage in one. Looking back, I know it would have done me good. I once had a summer job in which I sat in a windowless room, waiting for the phone to ring so that I could take tee-time reservations for a golf course. This was Monday through Saturday, eight hours per day. I read J. R. R. Tolkien's *Lord of the Rings* and Alex Haley's *Roots*, and played about a million games of solitaire. If only I had known how to knit!

Finally, in the summer of 1999, when I knew I was going to be traveling a lot and spending interminable hours in airports, I decided I needed something worthy and portable to keep myself busy. The clincher was that the local Wal-Mart was for some reason liquidating its entire stock of knitting supplies. I am hopelessly attracted to bargains, and with needles going for fifty cents and skeins going for a dollar or two, I bought the incredibly cheesy "I Taught Myself Knitting" kit by Boye and decided to puzzle it out before traveling.

My first project was the one the Boye booklet recommended: a garter-stitch scarf. I completed casting on without a problem, the pictures being very clear and helpful. Though left-handed, I followed the directions for right-handers (as the booklet suggested) and engaged in English-style knitting. I'd knit for a bit, find holes and unaccountable increases and decreases, rip it all out, and start anew. I don't remember being frustrated, since this was further than I'd ever gotten before. And I was doing it all by myself. When I was about halfway along, I took my knitting to a friend's house. Everyone else there was playing bridge, and I sat nearby, persevering with my scarf. One of the bridge players, Shirleen, watched me for a while and then came over to helpfully adjust and direct my needle action. My product had been satisfactory, but I was achieving it in a very awkward way. Shirleen became my early mentor, and I would go to her to decipher the imponderables of knitting directions.

I do not come from a knitting family, though my maternal grandmother was an avid crocheter. She died when I was eight years old, however, so I do not think there was much influence there. When I was growing up, my mother never engaged in crafts for crafts' sake. Making things was a practical and thrifty answer to some need. When our furniture needed upholstering, she learned to upholster. When chairs needed re-caning, she learned how to cane. Not until recently has she started to invest herself in activities in order to *create*. She now quilts and makes floorcloths, and these are forms of self-expression, not mere furnishings. She is discovering art and color and texture, and in doing so, I think she is exploring a part of herself and her world that she has never known. I think that my own full—fanatical?—engagement with knitting is also in answer to some need to create and express. Both my mother and I have come to places where we have the luxury to invest time and effort (and, yes, money) in that exploration, rather than just meeting basic needs of food and shelter.

I have been knitting nonstop since I learned. I knit every day; I cannot imagine not doing so. I am constantly trying new techniques—which, looked at practically, is silly, since I could stick with what I know (or do) best and produce a better product. But I much prefer challenging projects: new stitches, intricate patterns, and multiple colors and fibers, though these challenges are not always successful. I have a little pile of failed projects (*many* lone socks, for example), which have taught me much. It is not about the product. It is about creation and balance and patience and learning. I want to keep learning, and I want to master the fundamentals. I am thinking about taking The Knitting Guild of America's course, during which the students are guided and assessed in different areas; maybe this will force me into mastery. Or maybe just time and love of the craft are enough to ensure progress. Right now, my contentment and excitement and passion come from discovery, but perhaps one day it will be enough just to knit.

I'll knit anything that presents itself. I have a long list of things I want to knit but haven't yet. Just today, I decided that I really *need* to knit: 1) a hot-water bottle cover, 2) a polar bear toy, 3) a necktie, 4) another sofa cushion, 5) a cotton top (for my boss's birthday in one week), 6) Norwegian mittens, 7) a tea cozy, and 8) a plastic grocery bag mosaic wall hanging. That's just today's list—at least the bits I can remember. (I should clarify that I do work full-time, in a mostly non-knitting environment, and cannot possibly make all the things I want to. Woe is me.)

I do it every evening: after work, dinner, dishes, no matter how I feel. I knit at the dining room table, the WIP [work-in-progress] basket on the floor, a big boom box on the table to play my latest book on tape, headphones on my head so that my husband can read and listen to the nightly symphony broadcasts on public radio in the adjoining living room. A rather funny picture, but I relish my evening knitting time. If I am feeling down, it helps me feel better. If I am feeling up, I feel great. I think its rhythmic, steady, progressive nature is a wonderful tonic. Choosing fibers and colors, adapting or creating patterns—is it empowerment that I feel? Energy? Calm, empowering energy? Calm, empowering, energizing joy? Whatever it is, it is also an addiction. I do it because I must.

I think the joy of it comes with the first concrete steps: finding a pattern, choosing the yarn. But I am impatient until I have actually cast on and begun to knit. Even checking the gauge sometimes feels like backpedaling. I get impatient to go, go, go—an irony, since I have assumed that knitting is teaching me patience.

I am really good at guilt and at "shoulds": I should learn continental knitting. I should know how to crochet for necklines and borders. I should spend more time learning how to properly sew seams and finish off a garment. I should master multiple color usage on double-pointed needles. I should try something with a zipper in it. I should try entrelac. I should memorize a basic sock pattern.

I have been assuming that the above will work their way into my knitting when they are ready. I hope so.

There are some great teenage students in the evening knitting activity I run at school. One is a Russian girl, Valentina, who is an absolute master at needlecraft. She is as experienced as anyone I have ever seen, and she is less than twenty years old. How she got that experienced in so short a time is a mystery. She knits and crochets prolifically, designing her own garments, never following a pattern—disdaining these, because they seldom use the "right" (i.e., the easiest, the most efficient, the prettiest) technique. She also sews and embroiders and weaves. She is an old soul at working with fiber, and she is the voice of wisdom in the activity.

Another girl is Norwegian, and I think knitting is in her DNA. She entered the activity as a beginner and took to it like breathing. She promptly began designing her own projects, embarking on the kind of straight-from-the-head, adventurous knitting that one day I hope to be able to do. She is not the grandmotherly teacher that Valentina is; she is the "naughty" knitter of bikinis and sports bras who rejoices in going her own way and figuring it all out for herself.

Knitting in a multicultural community is fascinating, since one can see how the craft has developed and how it is taught around the world. Bhutanese knitting looks nothing like German knitting, though the product is very much the same. One of the most interesting things in the group is hearing about how knitting is regarded in different places around the world. In some cultures, for example, weaving and fiberwork are the man's domain. Several of the students have gone home and surprised their families with their newly learned skill. The students, in turn, are also surprised when their mother or grandmother, whom they've never seen knit, suddenly unearths a stash of yarn and needles and begins to teach and share with them. It is also fun to see what they bring back from home—the yarns and the different kinds of needles. I suspect that for the male knitters, there might be a bit of rebellion in their decision to learn how to knit. In Senegal, for example, it is very much a woman's craft, and I am not sure that Mohammed will knit when he goes home. The "philosophy" behind his decision to knit may be to just experience something that belongs to a different realm.

Since I started knitting, I have taught many people how to do it. There are great reasons to learn knitting: it is not difficult; it is productive; it need not be expensive; it is portable; it requires no electricity or special equipment; it is profoundly joyful (at least for me). It slows us down, so that we must sit still and experience ourselves and the action being taken. But it is not a passive activity, like watching television or shopping at the mall; it does not dull minds but sharpens them and makes them keen. It stops us from consuming and allows us to create instead. And with knitting, you can use and reuse materials: old sweaters can be reknit into new ones; mistakes can be unraveled and redone; anything long and vaguely stringlike can be turned into something via knitting. I think knitting has value for everyone; the more of us who engage in creative and mindful activities such as this, the more quality and meaning our lives and our culture take on.

 It occurred to me after reading Elizabeth's letter that some of the students in her knitting activity might agree to answer questions from me. Elizabeth introduced me to three of them via e-mail. Lani Visaisouk, who in the summer travels home from school to her family in the Netherlands, was the first to respond. Then came Jen Spanier, a native of Illinois and, in some ways, Lani's polar opposite as a knitter. Finally, Valentina Katchanovskaya, the "needlecraft master" Elizabeth referred to in her letter, who wrote to me from her native city of St. Petersburg, Russia.

Each time I discovered a new e-mail in my inbox, I found myself giddy in anticipation of what its contents would yield. What stories would it unfold? What mysteries of knitting would it elucidate? As for the knitters who wrote these missives to me, it seemed that no matter where on earth they hailed from, they were never surprised or perplexed by the questions I asked. And, reading their letters, I was never disappointed by their answers.

LANI VISAISOUK

How gratifying it is to see one's family warmly, comfortably, and even fashionably dressed, in garments that really fit them. . . .

—ELIZABETH ZIMMERMANN,

KNITTING WITHOUT TEARS, 1971 (1995)

I'm a knitting misfit—barely out of my teens. Outside of the United World College, I've never met anyone my age who knits. I'm also unreliable on finishing large projects, such as sweaters. If I feel like knitting something, I might begin but never finish if it's something larger than mittens. I am a constant source of hope and annoyance to my mother, who has been wishing for a sweater since I was ten, but has not yet received one.

As a five-year-old, I was desperate to learn to knit after seeing craft-book projects and handknit garments made by family friends. However, only when my aunt moved to the Netherlands from New Zealand was I given the chance to learn at the age of six or seven. I began with purple wool on crooked needles, full of enthusiasm. Although I remember (oddly enough) suddenly having more stitches on the needle than I started out with, I remember knitting as fairly simple and an unending source of fun; this attitude probably stemmed from the fact that one of my greatest dreams at the time had been fulfilled. Most of my projects were scarves or dolls' clothes knit with scrap wool and with a vision of the finished product, though no pattern, in mind.

Although I was an enthusiastic knitter at first, the glory of knitting scarves began to wear off, and by the time I was eleven, I had stopped altogether. My interest was rekindled at UWC when Elizabeth and our German teacher founded the ever-popular knitting activity. My style and method have changed as I've learned new techniques—for example, the ability to knit in the round and produce socks and mittens rather than flat garments. I now see knitting as less of an opportunity to dress dolls than to dress people. Scarves tend to bore me, as do the general sock and mitten. Though it sounds vain, I knit to show off what I can do—especially complex Norwegian Selbu patterns. Rather than for Barbies, now I knit for the people I love, and as a rule I knit a pattern only once. By doing so, I can be sure that everyone has something unique.

Overall, my perception of what I can do with needles and wool, as well as what can be done with the finished product, has definitely changed; rather than being utilitarian, my projects are meant to demonstrate both affection and skill.

For me, knitting is an act of love. Granny Joyce, my surrogate grandmother, was a prolific and skilled knitter for decades before she put away the knitting needles to do needlepoint. She regularly knitted sweaters for each grandchild (including me and my brother) and kept careful track of whose turn it was. She knit out of love for her family—seven Cowichan Indian sweaters one year for Christmas presents, and she was working on them until four in the morning on Christmas Day. The sweater tags always said MADE SPECIALLY FOR YOU BY GRANNY JOYCE.

I find socks and mittens more personal gifts than scarves, perhaps because they must be sized to the person. For my best friend's seventeenth birthday, I knitted him Norwegian socks. I know that he does not understand the significance of the pattern (Norwegian gods) or fully appreciate the aesthetic aspect of these socks. The joy in the project came from knowing that he would wear them in the winter, and that he would be able to show them off, telling his family, "Lani made these for me"—a most unusual gift of love.

Since I want all gifts to be personal, I usually give a lot of thought to the aesthetics of a project. Just dreaming of and planning a project makes me happy, perhaps because I anticipate the end reactions from the recipients. Selecting the pattern, picking out the wool, testing the gauge, and finally Kitchener-stitching the sock toes together all involve the same amount of joy, although I am generally *relieved* to be finished with a project.

I follow Dale of Norway patterns or mock-Norwegian patterns from other companies. I don't usually design my own, although I might take a Dale motif from a sweater and adapt it to socks or mittens. In following patterns, what I most enjoy is the regularity and precision with which I must knit. In these certainties, there is a kind of comfort: The only mistakes will be my own follies. Surfing the Internet, I inevitably come across amazing knitters who churn out one Norwegian ski sweater per month. I look for such photographs to inspire me, although their influence is probably suspect, since I have yet to knit such a sweater.

Knitting seems to be a dying art, even in Europe. There are very few stores that sell high-quality wool and even fewer people who are willing to share their knitting knowledge, at least in the Netherlands. Moreover, the price of quality wool in the United States is soaring, and in many instances it's cheaper to buy the finished product rather than make it yourself. I think that knitting is already something of a relic, an act that the younger generation finds a curiosity but not cool enough to learn.

JEN SPANIER

*Perhaps you have heard of the woman
who had knit fifteen socks, but who
had yet to finish a pair?*

—GERTRUDE WHITING,

OLD-TIME TOOLS AND TOYS

OF NEEDLEWORK, 1928 (1971)

Elizabeth taught me to knit less than two years ago. I hated it at first: It all seemed so frustrating and complicated. It's kind of funny that an activity that I now find so relaxing used to give me headaches. My first project was a square—just a plain square to put under a plant—to see if I could knit straight.

No one in my family knits, though all the women crochet, so I'm kind of breaking a pattern. I think that knitting is considered to be a very conventional female activity, so it seems to me that when I do it, I should be sitting in an old rocking chair in front of a fireplace with children at my feet, rather than in my dorm room.

I actually don't knit outside of school. Maybe it's my method of procrastination from my studies, and that's why I don't need to knit on vacation. My style is still pretty much the same as when I started, but it's gotten more loose and comfortable; I don't have to fight the yarn as much. I never knew the things that could be done with knitting needles—I've even knit with plastic bags since I learned. Still, I knit mostly scarves. This is partly because I'm a slow knitter and partly because I made a scarf for my significant other and now everyone wants one. I can start the scarves in January and have all of them ready for Christmas. But I knit more for myself than others, usually only things that I can make out of rectangles, such as fingerless gloves, scarves, or bags. I also rarely finish a project—I just become involved in starting something else. I have a lot of half-done things at home.

Honestly, I knit because I'm restless—I like to keep my hands busy. Knitting is not only fun, it's also relaxing. You can sit and daydream while you knit, or listen to music, and not feel like you're being unproductive. It's a great stress-buster and, like I said, a great way to procrastinate. Also, you think to yourself (as a college student), *It's way cheaper to make this and a lot more fashionable than something I could buy.* It's very uplifting to look great and spend less money, especially when all the money you do have needs to go to tuition.

I would like people to know that since I learned to knit at eighteen—and picked up other crafts as a result—you can learn to do anything at any age, despite how weird others may think it is.

VALENTINA KATCHANOVSKAYA

[Y]ou can create something that has never been seen before. Time spent doing that is time well spent, in anyone's book.

—BARBARA WALKER,

CHARTED KNITTING DESIGNS, 1972

My grandma is the only one who knits in our family. Maybe it is because she had tuberculosis when she was twenty, and knitting was the only thing she was allowed to do in the hospital and the rehabilitation clinics. Except for her, I am the only one who knits now, so in a way I can call myself her successor.

My first knitting experience is something I still remember. I was seven years old, a lively child, not troubled by the political problems of my country. I used to spend all my vacations with my grandma, and because she is an excellent knitter, my wish to learn how to knit seems obvious. Grandma thought that dealing with two needles at the same time might be complicated for me, so first she taught me how to crochet. My first project was a funky dress for my tiny doll. I remember that it was fun at the beginning, but after ten minutes it became extremely boring. So, for the next year, the pattern of my knitting activity was the same: I started the project, and then Grandma had to finish it. But with time I was getting better. I stopped losing stitches, and the stitches became more even and pretty. When I got a Barbie doll for my birthday, she became the one I knitted for.

When I started, knitting was just a way of killing time during my long vacations; then it was a way of making pretty outfits for my Barbie, because it was impossible to buy any in Russia (my doll was brought from the United Kingdom by my friend's father). It was 1993, and my mother tried very hard to find clothes for my sister and me; I could not even think of asking her to buy anything for the doll. When I turned fifteen, my dolls were not that interesting anymore, so I started crocheting—mostly useful things, such as handkerchiefs. During my two years of high school I did not have any spare time, but I started knitting again at the United World College.

Is it possible to stop learning at all? I don't think so. The same is true for knitting. You can always find something new in the ways of knitting, in yourself while knitting, or in your attitude toward knitting. Sometimes, the thing does not come out right, and you have to break down the thing you just finished; or, if you are out of ideas, knitting can teach you patience or provoke your creativity. Every new project is a challenge to me, no matter how complicated it is.

I started knitting for myself not so long ago. Actually, I mostly knit for other people. For instance, I made socks for all my friends, but I still do not have my own pair. I make small things, such as gloves, mittens, scarves, and socks, that I give away. The only thing I ever knit for myself was a scarf that I made on an airplane.

I think I need to knit all the time. I need a mood for knitting—I call it a knitting mood. I can be sad or merry; it does not matter at all. When

I am having a bad day, I start making something completely crazy, like red socks with yellow stars (don't laugh—I really made them). But when I am feeling fine, I can do anything. Knitting gives me time and a chance to think, because my thoughts are free while knitting, so I can daydream or do some planning.

The ideas come to me at very random times; I can be solving differential equations or working out on a treadmill or even talking to somebody. Once, I saw a strange leaf; it was a huge greenish-red thing. A week later, I made another pair of socks with the same strange and beautiful combination of colors and patterns. When I get excited about a new project, I want to start it straight away, no matter what I have to do or where I have to go. Starting is always exciting and thrilling. While making the middle part, my project can change several times and become something completely different. By the time I finish the project, I start to hate it, just because I've looked at it too often. So I have to put it away for some time (usually a week), and when I take it out, I start to like it again. A week after, I start to like it enough to give it to somebody.

While lurking around *Knitter's Review*, I also came across Jessica Droeger, a thirty-seven-year old lawyer and mother of two who lives in Chicago. An excerpt from her post, which propelled me instantly to contact her: "I think people think it's funny that I knit, not because of my age but because of my occupation. Maybe they think we're all either bookworms or power-lunchers, or maybe they think we have no creativity, so how could we possibly like something so artsy? I think I love knitting because I so desperately need a creative outlet after reviewing (and, OK, writing) boring documents most of the day."

We debated, Jessica and I, whether I should actually interview her by phone, but she admitted she was wary of winging her answers and also warned me that, if I were to call to talk to her at home, her kids would "for sure want to say hi to you and I'll never get the phone back without a lot of yelling on all our parts." I had to admit, that sounded just fine to me, but eventually we opted to e-mail instead. And as the hot New York summer months dragged on and on, we continued to e-mail. I would tell her about my progress on the book; she told me about what was going on—knitwise and not—in her life in Chicago.

JESSICA DROEGER

Clothes for the new baby! Nothing makes us feel more strongly the marvel of a single human life and at the same time wonder at the myriad lives which have peopled the earth. The mother who to-day plans the daintiest of layettes is, in spirit, doing what millions of other mothers in many centuries have done.

—The Modern Priscilla magazine, 1917–1918

I taught myself how to knit in high school. As part of a project based on Thoreau's *Walden,* we had to make something for ourselves that we would otherwise usually buy. I decided to knit a sweater. I still have it—a fairly simple stockinette-stitch cotton sweater. It's a bit yellowed with age at this point. I remember my mom being impressed because I was able to knit with fairly consistent stitches right off the bat, while she would be all over the place, sometimes knitting too tightly and sometimes too loosely. It made me feel good, because my mom is an artist and very creative. I didn't feel I inherited her creativity gene like my brothers did. I couldn't draw, but at least I could make something pretty in my own way.

I basically stopped knitting after that—I'm not sure exactly why. Being busy with a new life may have been the biggest reason, having no truly disposable income may have been another (although when I was in college, I always had money for pizza and beer, but that's another discussion). I also used to be a much more social creature than I am now. Whenever I had free time, I was fairly intent on filling it up with socializing, probably to prevent myself from actually thinking about the various problems and issues I had in my life; my then-frail psyche couldn't handle too much soul-searching. Since I didn't know anyone who knit, it would have been a fairly solitary thing. I think that's one of the reasons I crave knitting now—it's almost purely time just for me.

Recently, I felt a strong desire to be creative again. I thought I would take up needlepoint, but while I was looking for info on needlepoint on the Internet, I stumbled upon *Knitter's Review*. Seeing all the enthusiasm for knitting on its online forum renewed my own enthusiasm. I've been knitting now since about November of last year, and I would say (and my husband would probably agree) that I'm addicted. Since I've been reading the *KR* forum, my view of the possibilities of knitting has expanded enormously—I had never thought about knitting socks before, for instance (although I haven't tried it yet), and I had never thought of using double-pointed or circular needles for straight knitting.

I tend to spend more time working on projects for other people than for myself. I'm more conscientious about those things; if there's an error in something for me and it's not really noticeable, I might not fix it, but if I made the same error in something for someone else, I'd agonize over it until it was fixed. I really love the feeling of giving handmade items to people—I like making baby things, because having a baby is such a special occasion that it deserves a special gift—and even though I like wearing my own creations (or would if I ever had time to finish any of the projects for myself), I feel good when I'm working on things for other people. It doesn't feel as selfish that way.

I knit whether I'm happy or sad, tired or stressed out—I hate doing nothing. Since I have so many projects going at once, I can pick up whatever feels right at the moment. (Currently I have in progress a baby blanket and sweater, an afghan for my husband, and a scarf and sweater for myself.) Now that I think about it, I guess I tend to pick up my husband's afghan after we've had a fight. It could be a whole subconscious thing—that I somehow feel I'm mending the relationship—but more likely, I do it because I feel like I'm doing something nice for him and for me at the same time.

I am a slave to patterns. I am also a slave to recipes, which I think is rooted in the same fear: I don't trust my own judgment when it comes to things someone else might wear or eat. I also think that I'm just not an advanced enough knitter to improvise in most cases. Perhaps once I better understand different kinds of sweater construction, for instance, I might be able to mix and match sleeve or collar types in different patterns to make something I like more. I would also like to be able to substitute yarns more effectively, but I don't have the base knowledge of fiber types, how they look when knit, how they wear, and their various gauges to be able to do that without a lot of help. I don't mind following a pattern, though. The finished product is still mine, even if I didn't conceive the pattern on my own.

I wish I could say that my knitting is influenced by the colors of Monet paintings or a summer sunset, but I'm not that creative. My knitting is inspired more by my desire to relax, not so much by what I envision the finished product to be. I really want to do cables, but I haven't since my early, early knitting days. I think it will make my knitting look more interesting, but I'm a little worried that I'll have to concentrate too much to get them right, so I haven't tried them yet. I think the same goes for other things, like knitting with more than one color, but eventually I will do that, too, once I feel more confident and get bored with the kinds of things I'm working on now.

I *would* knit anywhere, anytime, but I'm usually in a place (for example, at work) where I simply can't knit. I suppose I could bring it with me and do it at lunch, but I don't know how that would be received. I take it with me when the family goes on vacation or when I take my daughter to ballet class, for instance, and I try to steal a little time to knit here and there. Recently, on a Saturday afternoon, both my girls fell asleep in their car seats on the way home. Since we live in a high-rise, I couldn't leave them in the garage or get them inside our apartment without waking them, so I sat there in the car and knit for an hour while they slept. It wasn't the most comfortable place, and the light wasn't great, but it was wonderful to have the time and quiet just the same.

Knitting, for me anyway, is a giving art; it's art that's meant to be shared with others. The knitters I know who embody that spirit are some of the women from the *KR* online forum. Clara, the hostess of the site, is someone who embodies the ethos of knitting for me. She shares her love of knitting with lots of people and seems like a wonderful, caring person. (When I once posted that I couldn't find a particular magazine, she offered to send me an extra copy that she picked up at the store.) She spins her own yarn and knits with all kinds of different yarns and then shares her experiences, allowing people like me to learn. I hope someday to teach my daughters to knit, since it's really the only creative thing I feel confident doing. I'd like to think I passed on to them a practical pastime that they can do their whole lives, regardless of where they live or the state of their health.

I feel as though I need to clarify some things about myself. I really like my job, so it's not like knitting is something I wish I could do for a living. I don't want to leave you with the impression that I'm somehow unfulfilled in other areas of my life; I actually have a really nice life. But before I started knitting again, I felt empty somehow. I felt a strong need to be artistic, and I'm just not good at some of the more traditional artsy things like drawing or painting—and it's not like I haven't tried. When I knit, I can make pretty things, and that makes me feel really good. Also, knitting is often associated with warmth. The last gift I gave was a bunch of soft, furry scarves to a friend with thyroid cancer. She calls them her "hugs" and says she puts them on when her throat needs a hug.

And another thing: I think knitting makes me feel like I'm not trendy, which makes me feel independent, like I'm the kind of person who follows her own path. No one in my crowd knits (OK, I don't really have a "crowd"), and I think people think it's funny for a lawyer to knit. I like surprising people—I don't want anyone to think they have me fig-ured out. I don't want to be a stereotype.

Knitting grounds me, helps me feel like I'm doing something real and tangible when all day I work with intangibles. Writing this made me think of a song by the Indigo Girls that talks about getting out of bed, using a hammer and a nail, and learning how to use your hands instead of your head. My knitting needles are the equivalent of that song's hammer and nail. Knitting is my refuge, my retreat from the world. Maybe one of the reasons I like making things for other people is that, in a strange way, it allows me to retreat without losing my connection to the person for whom I'm knitting.

There's been a lot of talk about how hip knitting is these days. Fads come and go—knitting probably won't be so hip in a couple years, and I think some of the interest is likely to fade when the next trend comes around. But for me, I don't see it as something that I'll give up anytime soon. I see it as a hobby I can take with me through retirement. (I'm only thirty-seven, but you have to plan for the future.) It's something I'll be able to do no matter what the state of my health is. There will always be yarn and knitting needles.

Of course, it was thanks to *Knitter's Review*, which really is an excellent, informative, and well-organized website, that I was able to meet all the people who precede this entry. And yet it wasn't until I decided that I wanted to quote directly from the first online forum posts I'd read by Elizabeth and Jessica that I thought to contact Clara Parkes, the hostess of the site. Not only was she enthusiastic about members of her forum receiving mentions, she proved an invaluable resource to me as knitters' e-mails trickled in, filled with all sorts of knitting-specific abbreviations that were unfamiliar to me, like TKGOA (The Knitter's Guild of America), WIPs (works in progress), and UFOs (unfinished objects). Finally, I asked her to tell me a bit of her own story.

CLARA PARKES

*Knitting should be done thoughtfully.
It should not be hurried. That is
its charm to our generation, who
live surrounded with a wild
helter-skelter of speed. It is creative,
and that is its supreme satisfaction.*

—MARY THOMAS, *MARY THOMAS'S
KNITTING BOOK,* 1938 (1972)

I began developing the *Knitter's Review* website in early 1999 and launched it in September of the same year. At the time, the blog phenomenon hadn't yet hit. Online resources for knitting consisted primarily of free pattern collections, a few quarterly magazines, link directories, yarn shops, and e-mail lists. There really wasn't anything substantive to tide people over between issues of the quarterly print magazines. Meanwhile, yarn shops were taking their businesses online by the dozens, which meant a whole new universe for all of us. The only problems were 1) finding the shops, 2) figuring out which ones were reliable, and 3) trusting a shop's description of various yarns without being able to feel them in person. Thus was born *Knitter's Review,* a weekly publication for the online knitter. With no vendor affiliations, I could be honest about yarns, tools, shops, you name it. The reception has been fantastic. In November 2001, when I knew we had enough of a critical mass to support them, I launched our online discussion forums. The time was right, and they've grown into a wonderful, safe, friendly community.

I used to live in San Francisco, lead a glorious high-tech editing life, and live in a huge apartment with a fireplace and parking. But by May 1998, I was totally burned out. Everything I did was cerebral; everyone I encountered seemed to be caught up in the high-tech craze and removed from reality. Conspicuous consumption was getting to me.

So I gave it all up and moved across the country to Maine. For six generations now, my family has had a summer place with land on Penobscot Bay, which is a truly gorgeous spot. I realized that I'd rather spend fifty-one weeks a year here and one week elsewhere than the other way around. It took several years to renovate the farmhouse in which I would live, and in the meantime I lived in Portland, Maine. Finally, in October 2001, I moved up here. I still spend three days a week down in Portland, and that's where the warehouse is for the *Knitter's Review* boutique. But my heart, my cat, my yarn, and my garden are here.

I still write for high-tech publications, but I've been gradually reducing the high-tech so I can focus more on *KR*. It's always been a free publication, with revenue coming from sponsorships and special promotions with publishers. But we've reached the point at which the energy and resources required to sustain and grow *KR* properly require a greater infusion of capital. Instead of charging for content, which would alienate a lot of people and reduce my subscriber base by at least 80 percent, I've decided to spin off a boutique that'll carry beautiful knitting-theme notecards, posters, journals, totes, mugs, and collectibles. There won't be an ounce of yarn or anything else I'd discuss editorially, so there's still a clean ethical line. My hope is that this will enable me to bring in more writers and expand the site even further.

Knitting and community—there's an interesting double-edged sword to this. On the one hand, you have the early American tradition of women gathering together to spin, knit, or weave items, normally for the benefit of an individual or the community. Today, however, many knitters are totally isolated. I've received e-mails from readers saying they thought they were completely alone until they found my site. For them, the ability to connect with people who fundamentally understand, who don't judge or make jokes, is priceless. Forget politics, forget social standing, forget skin color, ethnicity, or sexual orientation—that's not at all what it's about. I'm sure if you put a cross sample of us in a room together, you'd find a quite potentially explosive combination of differences, but somehow, within the context of knitting, it works. When the rest of the world seems to be falling apart, I pull my focus back onto the *Knitter's Review* community, and I have hope.

Knitting can be such a deep-rooted love, with so many intricate psychological and emotional components I can't begin to verbalize. When you meet another person and discover that he or she is a knitter, there's an instant moment of recognition, relaxation, and mutual understanding. All those formalities fly right out the window. It's wonderful.

My maternal grandmother taught me to knit when I was thirteen years old. I was having a horrible time adjusting to my new high school, and as a big treat my mother took us all back east to my grandparents' house for Christmas. We'd moved to Arizona a few years prior, and let's just say that the desert and I didn't agree. The setting at my grandparents' couldn't have been more perfect—a beautiful Colonial house in a

New England town, with snow on the ground, a fire in the fireplace, and my dear grandma teaching me to knit. I was immediately hooked. The easy repetitive motions combined with just enough of a puzzle to keep the shallow layer of my brain occupied was perfect. And it was an unbelievable high to watch a piece of knitted fabric emerge on the other side of the needles.

My knitting waxed and waned over the years, but it was always there when I needed it: to stay grounded in college, to ease homesickness when I was living in France, to show my brother just how much his new baby meant to me, and to calm my nerves when I was in the midst of renovating my old farmhouse, which was 70 percent over budget.

As for its relevance to my life, I wouldn't want to stand on a mountaintop and proclaim my identity, first and foremost, as a knitter. It'd be pretty high on the list, but it's not the only thing that defines me. Knitting is my main creative medium. I also play piano, garden, and write, but nothing beats being able to envelop yourself in the softness and warmth of your own creation.

For me, holding a project in my lap and knitting away is almost a primal sensation. I can see my grandma's hands in mine, I think of the countless generations of women who clothed entire families with their knitting, and I feel both connected and grounded. Perhaps it's the same way a fifth-generation farmer feels, looking out over the fields that have been tended by generations past and that will, hopefully, be tended by generations to come. It's easier to understand your place in the cycle.

Now What?

For the further one travels
The less one knows.
—*TAO TE CHING*

It only took a day or so for me to realize that I would never use the contents of the $10 bag of blended wool I'd bought at the yarn sale. So tantalizing when I was in the throes of the yarn jones—and starving before breakfast to boot—once I was home and fed, its patina of caramel revealed itself to be no color so luscious. What I had on my hands here were ten balls of mucusy-looking stuff—beige with a sickly tinge of pink—that made my skin appear sallow when I held it against my arm. Included in the bag were a few practice swatches and the back panel of an abandoned sweater; apparently someone else before me had had the same disgruntled reaction.

Still, I was loathe to admit an error in judgment. "Ten balls for ten dollars," I chanted in my most delighted (feigned) bargain-hunter voice to my husband, who looked decidedly nonplussed. I squirreled the bag away in the closet, where it cluttered up my shoe corner for several weeks. Then, quietly, I moved it to the outer hallway, the last stop in our household before ultimate discarding.

I was still enthusiastic about the two balls of merino, though. I set straight to working some of the brown yarn (thankfully still chocolatey-looking in the rational light of the day after) into squares, following di-

64

rections in a Barbara Walker pattern treasury that I'd borrowed from Elanor. Lozenge, a simple knit/purl pattern of "some antiquity," according to the book, knitted up into a squirmy-looking patch—like worms on dirt, I decided. Squared Check, which I realized too late required me to double the suggested multiple in order to achieve the full force of its geometric effect, was similarly un-thrilling. So much for the brown merino. But whether the drab swatching results were honestly the fault of the wool or my fault for picking patterns inappropriate to the material, I didn't even bother to contemplate; once disappointment leads to disinterest, there's no recovering from it. I cast the yarn and the swatches it had spawned into a deep drawer.

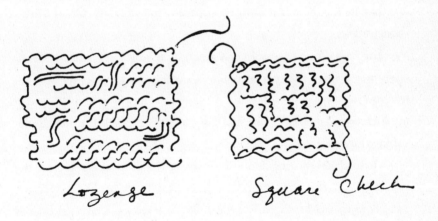

Lozenge   Square Check

But I had a very particular plan for the butter-yellow ball. My favorite sweater is a short, V-neck cardigan made of dark gray cashmere. After three years of wear, I had finally succeeded in loving it almost to death: Holes had been eaten out of it by both my elbows, and around the holes, the fabric was threadbare. I could not conceive of discarding this most perfect of all the world's sweaters. I needed to rescue it, give it a second life. Elbow patches struck me as just the thing.

Elanor, visiting for dinner one night, talked me out of knitting them. "What you want to do," she said, "is make your patches out of crochet." She rummaged around in her pocketbook and—Why? How?—emerged from it with a crochet hook. Too stunned to comment, I went to retrieve the yarn. With some hasty strokes, Elanor looped together a narrow chain, then handed the whole hook-and-wool operation over to me. I sat on a stool in my kitchen as dinner bubbled on the stove, and Elanor leaned on the counter, sipping wine and monitoring my progress, and in less than half an hour, I'd finished a three-inch oval. Easy. Or, at least, I thought it was.

The next day, I tried a second patch on my own. It somehow developed into a shriveled specimen that I quickly unraveled. My next attempt wasn't any more successful. I called Elanor, who told me to widen my increases—pick up more stitches—at the curves. I did, and the resulting third patch was . . . *not bad*.

Then came the moment of truth: sewing the patches onto the sweater. As I stitched, it became increasingly impossible to get the patches to lie flat. Furthermore, the yellow merino was a far sight thicker than the cashmere of my sweater, and the mingling of the two fabrics was decidedly ungainly. I finished sewing the patches on anyway, convincing myself that I was imagining things, that the patches—nice, even spirals of warm yellow—added a touch of panache to my beloved cardigan.

Once I tried the thing on, though, there was no denying the obvious: The patches protruded from my elbows like perfect, perky nipples.

elbow
patches

I resolved to wear the sweater anyway, always with my elbows bent to fill the contours of the patches. The yellow merino, which I'd planned to stash away with its brown cousin at the bottom of a drawer, met another, albeit accidental, fate: between the claws of my cat.

3.

Summer Days:
New York

Susan Haviland brought a huge assortment of knitted things to show me on the day we met at an East Village coffee shop, in a bag stuffed to virtual overflow: a turtleneck—cabled on the body, cuffs, neck, and hem—in a soft wool/alpaca blend; a tubular, cowlneck sweater in grayish-green mohair and silver rayon; a boxy pullover that featured a geometric pattern in which a series of multicolored stripes traveled first vertically on the front and back, then horizontally; a green triangular lace merino shawl; a shaggy "Janis Joplin" cape, fringed all over with metallic yarns; another finer merino shawl, this one gray and rectangular, featuring two columns of lace running down its surface; a cotton vest with a "little landscape" Fair Isle pattern; and a pair of blue cabled socks. No amount of exclaiming on my part seemed adequate enough in the face of such mastery.

I was introduced to Susan through Elanor. Elanor knows Susan through a Manhattan yarn shop—one of the oldest still existing there, and one my mother used to bring me to when I was a girl—that perches on the second floor of a building on lower Park Avenue, overlooking the squat, lovely limestone hulking of the Morgan Library. (Susan has since gone on to become design editor at Lion Brand Yarns.) "You will just love Susan," Elanor said to me, refusing to elaborate any further. Elanor lives in an apartment that is almost overrun by her creations and the materials necessary for making them. Cones of yarn hang from a large rack in her kitchen; stacks of fabric fill shelves; markers, needles, towers of empty cigar boxes—you encounter these things and many, many other things with every turn. The tables in her bedroom are covered with tchotchkes made of yarn or cardboard; knitted and sewn garments are draped over doors and chairs. As Susan pulled garment after garment out of her bag (which quickly began to remind me of those circus clown cars), how it was that she should rank among Elanor's favorite yarn store denizens seemed obvious: like minds—like knitters—attract.

SUSAN HAVILAND

*Knitting can truly be called a friend of
the aged and blind; the fingers sup-
plying the want of eyesight, and so-
lacing many weary hours which
otherwise be tedious to bear.*

—FLORENCE HARTLEY, *THE LADIES
HAND BOOK OF FANCY AND ORNAMENTAL
WORK—CIVIL WAR ERA, 1859 (1991)*

I started knitting in high school. I was sick, and I made something that
looked like it had been chewed. I remember pretty much figuring it
out on my own—how to make the edges and everything, and I finally
made a scarf. I thought it was no big deal; I just thought it was fun. And
that's still how I feel about knitting—I just think it's fun.

Then, when I was in college at Sarah Lawrence, I was in the theater,
and I knit because I had time on my hands—I was always hanging
around, waiting. You can't really read in those situations; you need to be
able to talk to people. In that respect, knitting is like worry beads. In my
twenties, I was moving around, doing my theater thing, totally impover-
ished. I knit, but again, it was not a big deal. It became a big deal later,
when I quit doing theater and started working in financial services and
needed a creative outlet. I discovered authors like Elizabeth Zimmerman and Barbara Walker, and suddenly knitting became very liberating

for me. I saw it as a craft more than something you just did to make a garment. It's a practical craft, too—it's how you use it in your life. It's also stretchy and sculptural, and it hugs the body. There's not a lot of artifice to it. It's clean.

When you knit, you're creating something, and any creative activity is empowering, because you're in charge; it's coming from you. We're taught things very much as if they're right or wrong—especially in knitting, when you're working from patterns—and that isn't helpful. When

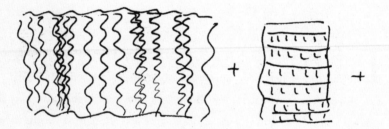

I teach, I want to let my students figure out everything on their own, but then there's something about tradition, too, that really cuts to the chase. There needs to be a balance, I think, between exploring the activity and having people wander around on their own. So when I teach, I talk a lot about the history of knitting and the importance of seeing what people before you have done. And I want my students to look at the world around them. We live in a man-made city, and I find that all kinds of little things from that environment come into my work: geometric forms, color and abstract patterns, textures.

I find it fascinating to see how people adapt to the craft of knitting. I look at other people's work—that fascinates me—and I look to see how something's done. I'm certainly more traditional than some people I know. Some people have a very strong personal style. I do, too, but I'm a little more eclectic; I like to try new things. I don't feel too heavily formed. People change, and whatever I'm doing at any given time is part of who I am at the moment. I don't think knitting happens in a straight line. What I do with it depends on what's happening in my life, and that

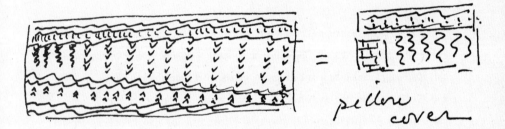

can be part of the fun of it. Who knows where you're going? You can go anywhere. I get some idea, and it takes me away.

I work on a lot of things at once, and I don't obligate myself to finish. That's part of the indulgence of knitting for me. I'll have a lace thing and a color thing and a cable thing, and now I'm doing two different things with feathers, one in a heavy yarn, one in kind of a medium yarn. I don't always like to knit with cashmere—I like a variety. Sometimes I want flashy and a little firm; sometimes I want very soft.

It's intuitive, what I decide to work on. If it's late at night, I'm not going to work on my lace, because it takes too much concentration. Sometimes, in the morning, I'm raring to go and I'm going to do this complicated thing, and I pull out all my yarns and play with colors for two hours and make swatches all day long. I may have nothing at the end of it, but I do get into these fervors. Sometimes I put my swatches together—and I encourage other knitters to do this, too—but it depends on how I'm feeling. Sometimes I want to use the yarn again, or I don't want the swatches cluttering up my already-cluttered life. Sometimes I make little mini-projects—sweaters or vests or panchos in quarter- or half-scale—when I just want to make something with the yarn.

There are a lot of people who knit in hospitals, or they take it up in times of stress, for example, when they have a parent dying in the hospital. Knitting can be helpful during a crisis, and I would say that's true for me—but maybe not as much as it was before I starting doing it professionally. On September 11, though, I lost one of my brothers, and I couldn't knit for a while; I couldn't do anything. And then I took it up again, but I couldn't do anything very creative. I just wanted to experience the tactile, mindless aspect of knitting. I didn't feel like laying myself on the line in any way, intellectually or emotionally. So I did a few patterns—I was knitting, but not to challenge myself, or to achieve any sort of status quo. Knitting can be what you want it to be. There are as many different kinds of knitters as there are people.

I live in a knitting factory. I'm a madwoman—I have yarn everywhere. I love to dream about yarn and about color. I've had dreams, too, where yarn was crashing down on me. Those chartered knitting books by

Barbara Walker are like the Bible to me. I look at them before I go to bed. Occasionally, I've invented some squiggly little thing that I'll incorporate into my knitting, but someone probably did it before me. I don't feel that territorial about my stuff. Just because it hasn't been published doesn't mean it hasn't been done before ever. You can take something and really go with it and make it yours that way. I think it's just a matter of how you put everything together.

I teach some senior citizens who do radical color work and some young people who are very traditional—pink things for girls and all stitches very tight. However you are is how you'll knit. But it doesn't matter. We're all creating something from within our own vision. One of the things that I like about knitting is that it's a shared activity—I don't like the idea of an age ghetto. Knitting can break through that. You don't need to be in great health—you can still knit. That's one reason I'm attracted to it. Other activities drop away as you age. After college, I used to read to a blind woman, and she was amazing. She would just feel things out. That's something that I practice—knitting with my eyes closed—to see what I can do with it. Or I turn the lights off. You get into the rhythm of it and the sensuality of touch, and you can feel it with your fingers. We're all so locked in to using our eyes. I think it's also good to smell your material a little bit, try to explore different aspects of the yarn. Cooking is like that—using your senses.

I was thinking about getting rid of everything I own that's not knitted—periodically I get that idea. I'd better get busy.

From Susan came Arlene Mintzer, who, when we met, was Susan's coworker and coteacher at the yarn shop on Park Avenue. We rendezvoused at a used bookshop in SoHo, which is housed in a space so cavernous that every sound echoes through it; most of our conversation hardly reached above a whisper, and in the time we spent together, huddled with our heads close together over mugs of tea, the topic of knitting took on a mysterious, subversive air.

For no reason that she could articulate, Arlene—a cheerful New York native with a warm twinkle in her eye—had decided that I would be averse to seeing great piles of her work. Her first impulse, she told me, had been to bring along with her, as Susan had, a bag packed to the gills with every variety of knitted item she could dig out of her drawers and closets. But she had studiously tailored her selection to three hats and one wood-handled handbag—tight, intricate things made from the combinations of angora, mohair, cotton, silk, wool, and alpaca she favors, and decorated with all manner of bobbles and beads. I could have stood, I told her, to see much more.

Arlene Mintzer

To knit creatively, you have only to let your imagination go.

—Barbara Walker, *A Second Treasury of Knitting Patterns*, 1970 (1998)

I have been involved with textile making since I was a child. I've always loved to go to the yarn store and buy yarn. We didn't have a car when I was growing up in Queens, New York, so every Saturday my grandfather would come pick us up, and he would take us to Brooklyn, and he would always give me a little bit of money to play with. I would hit the dime store and buy yarn all the time. Even now, I never get tired of it.

My mother taught me how to knit. It was frustrating because I'm extremely left-handed and I knit onto my left-hand needle, which is not the norm for most lefties. I was knitting backward—knitting into the back of the stitch and purl-scooping from the front, which is legitimate, but then I would get confused when a pattern said to knit through the back of the stitch. Later, when I was about sixteen, I had a friend named Beatrice. She and her family would invite me over in the evening, and we would eat Pop-Tarts, which now just make my teeth hurt, and we would knit. Beatrice, even though she was right-handed, was able to somehow correct the knitting for me so I wasn't so frustrated. And every time I would do something well she would go, "Arlene, that's *beauteous*." Slowly, my knitting evolved, and it's kept evolving.

I was a very serious crocheter for about ten years, from 1970 to1980. In the 70s, I wrote knitting and crocheting instructions for a major women's magazine—I was part of the how-to department. I had a wonderful mentor there. She was very patient in teaching me about garment construction. One day I went to her and said, "I really want to design," and she said, "That's great." And I asked, "But can you do *this* with *this*?" She looked and me and grinned and said, "Arlene, you can do anything with anything." It took me about ten years to realize what that meant, and I'm still exploring it. I would say now that ultimately I am a textile maker, but knitting is an incredibly important part of that. I do a lot of knitting in which I combine elements of crochet—there is a great, happy marriage between these two elements. I get the drape I want from knitting, but the crochet pulls it all together for me. I do a tremendous amount of accessory making—it pushes me. It's a real challenge; in a hat, say, you only have six or seven inches to make a statement.

Even though I was crocheting between 1970 and 1980, I was still knitting for my job, what they call "execution work," which is making garments that would be featured in the magazine. A designer would come in with a finished garment, but the magazine wanted to do it in another yarn, in another color, so they would ask me if I'd redo it. I became a hand-spinner, too, and a lot of the yarns I was spinning were too heavy for crochet—I needed another vehicle. Barbara Walker, in *A Second Treasury of Knitting Patterns,* has a technique called Swedish Weave, in which you weave a heavier yarn back and forth as you're knitting with a lighter ground yarn.* I had a customer who wanted to do a full-length

*Barbara Walker describes it like this: "In this pattern Color B is never worked, only passed back and forth between the needles as the knitting is done with Color A."

coat, and she was about six feet tall, and she wanted to do it in her hand-spun. I said, "Well, this is going to be extremely expensive; let me think of a way for you to use the hand-spun and combine it with a commercial yarn." The Swedish Weave took over, because you could lay the hand-spun over the other yarn. After that, I became totally obsessed with knitting.

Swedish Weave to me is the most Zen form of knitting I have ever done. You can make beautiful fabric from it and there isn't any type of yarn you can't use. It's also a good indicator of how the knitter is really feeling. If you're very tense, the work pulls in; if you're very relaxed, the work loosens; and if you're feeling even-tempered, the fabric remains very symmetrical.

I think deep down inside, I'm really a painter at heart, but I would much rather paint with yarn than with pigment. The idea of taking string and making it into a beautiful piece of fabric that can also be wearable is a huge turn-on for me. I'm also an animal lover, so I like the idea that the fibers came from a llama, say, and it didn't have to be killed. My great-est pleasure is to go to a museum. I saw the exhibit of Pierre Bonnard paintings at The Metropolitan Museum of Art six times. The inspiration that comes from fine art can be translated into knitted fabric. One hat that I made was very much influenced by the Bonnard show. It's an ex-ample of Swedish Weave, done with hand-dyed rickrack. For me to do a solid-colored whatever at this point, I don't think I could handle it.

I believe there can be great artistry in the way someone makes some-thing—*anything*. It happens whenever you take the basics and push them to a level that is unique and somehow infuse your creation with a great deal of your own individual passion to the point at which someone says,

"I never would have thought of that." Even if you've never designed anything on your own, if you've taken a fisherman's pattern and chosen your yarn, who's to say that is any more or less important than designing it yourself? There's a certain sense of excellence, in which technique is important, but I don't think one should be so obsessed with technique that true creativity is limited. I was trained to be very technical and proficient, but for so many years I've been telling everyone to break the rules and have fun with it. But I think to myself, *Can you do this?*—I have this dialogue with myself—and then I say, "Of course you can do it; the knitting police aren't coming after you."

I have many wonderful textile-related jobs, but my favorite is teaching at Parson's School of Design in New York City—I teach a knitting elective to undergrad fashion design students. They are my flower garden. I teach them basic knitting, but I have them for fifteen weeks. I keep saying to them, "I want you to learn the basics, and then I want you to do anything and everything that you possibly can." The students are thrilled; they love coming to knitting class. They realize, too, that there's a lot of hard work involved to get from A to B, but by the end of the semester, I feel like I've really opened up that world for them. I get to share my passion, and it doesn't get any better than that. I get to be excited all over again.

You're not building a suspension bridge when you're knitting. Whatever you do when you knit can be undone if you don't like it, so there's no reason to be fearful of the ramifications. I think women in general tend to be more timid about learning how to knit. When a man begins a knitting class and he drops a stitch, so what? Women are more intimidated; there's a sense of perfectionism from the get-go, and that shouldn't be the case. I'm always reminding students, "If you drop a stitch, so what? I'm not going to teach you how to fix it the first night, because there are more important things that we have to do."

You can paint with yarn and needles. If people would let themselves relax, they'd find that knitting can ultimately give them a great deal of creative expression. I was once teaching a workshop out of town, and there was this woman sitting at the back of the room. She had these beautiful blue eyes, and she was looking very intent. At the end of the day I asked her, "Are you alright?" And she started to cry, tears streaming down her face. I asked, "Did I offend you? Was it something I said?" She said, "No, but no one's ever given me this much creative freedom before." That was amazing to me. It was very touching. She had felt very unsafe and wasn't quite ready to go where I wanted her to.

I'd like to say to my students, "Give yourself permission to try this—you'll be amazed." Some of the best work I've done I first thought, *You can't do this.* Or I did something differently by accident. If you don't try, you don't know. But I also want people to be relaxed when they're knitting, mindful of whether their shoulders are up around their ears or not, and I tell students, "When you get mad at your knitting, put it down and go do something else. Ask yourself, 'What if I try this, and what if I try that?' Give yourself permission, because you *can.*" Probably the greatest gift anyone ever gave me in my work was: "You can do *anything* with *anything.*"

How to Do Everything

What we are today comes from our thoughts of yesterday, and our present
thoughts build our life of tomorrow: Our life is the creation of our mind.

—*The Dhammapada*

I had learned my lesson about impulse yarn shopping (to be remembered, probably, only until I came across the next yarn sale), but a
more important idea was beginning to dawn on me. "How you do anything is how you do everything," one knitter I met said to me, and the
implications of this with regard to knitting—and what, exactly, I was
hoping to accomplish with it—were becoming clearer.

For years, as long as I can remember, I've cooked, written, painted,
taken photographs, and made all manner of ornately decorated boxes
and cards. And for each of these things, I've built up a sort of mental catalog of useful information that I can draw from. With cooking, for example, I've read and experimented with thousands of recipes, and bits
and pieces of them—techniques, and memories of what flavors work
well with others—are now ingrained in my memory. The knowledge I've
accumulated from everything I've cooked before dictates what—and
how—I cook now. In short, I've done my research, and that research
makes everything else possible.

What does this have to do with knitting? After that day in Elanor's
kitchen, when I had my first real revelation about knitting—that it was
really only two stitches with a few variables thrown in—I made up my

mind that I wanted to expand my understanding of that one simple idea, much the same way I once set about understanding the various aspects of cooking. The only question was, How?

Not with garments—of that, at least, I was certain. Ever since I was a teenager, I've been amassing folders of pictures from magazines of sweaters and skirts and necklaces I hoped to one day make for myself. Flipping through the clippings in these folders sometime after that afternoon at Elanor's, all the knitted things struck me as extraordinarily dull and simplistic. The Fendi sweater that had once looked like the most gorgeous of garments I now understood to be constructed of a very basic stockinette stitch with extra-wide ribbing at the cuffs and hem; and the ribbing I now understood to be a simple matter of alternating knit and purl stitches. I suddenly couldn't imagine a less engrossing sweater to try to make.

There was another problem with garments: math. I am an admittedly shoddy craftsperson when it comes to measuring; no matter how diligently I apply myself, my math is always off by crucial, aggravating increments—this is why I don't sew. I'm one of those unfortunates who had a math genius in the family—my father, a rocket scientist, whose "help" with my math homework all throughout my school career always resulted in fits of tears on my part. He instilled in me a lifelong horror of math; I sometimes wonder how it is that I can even count at all. To make even the simplest knitted garment and have it fit was certainly going to require more skill than I possessed.

A final consideration had to do with my various fetishes—not just the one I'd been developing for yarn lately, but others for ribbon and fabric and pretty printed paper. I collect these things in enormous shopping bags that I cram onto the shelves of my closet. Presumably, I am collecting these things to use them—the fabric for making pillows and covering chair seats, the paper and ribbon for decoupaging or collaging. Every time I dive into one of my shopping bags, I find myself practically paralyzed. To use some of the fabric for a pillow, say, will result in a large gash in the remaining yardage, an ugly wound that will make my heart sink every time I see it, no matter how much pleasure the ensuing pillow might provide me. If I began to use the ribbon or the paper, I would eventually use them up—an unacceptable eventuality. This is a sickness; I know it, but I'm powerless to change it. The bags pile up and expand in size and in number year after year. But from this knowledge of myself comes another lesson: If I really was going to knit and not just collect yarn, I was going to have to figure out something—if not sweaters or other wearables—to use it for, something that would also provide a means for learning about the scope and possibilities of knitting.

And what I finally hit upon was swatching. I reached this conclusion with the help of Barbara Walker's pattern collections (in spite of my ambivalence for those early brown merino bits). Every small photo of every sample pattern in them looks to me like a square of patterned paper or cloth, gorgeous in its own right and unspeakably alluring (at least, to someone suffering from my particular illness). More than that, every photo of every pattern is like a tiny world unto itself, replete with its own rules and language; and all the patterns together make up a whole wide universe, one of terrific potential and variety as seemingly infinite as a starry night sky. I started marking my favorite pages in the book, dreaming that I would knit every pattern that intrigued me until I had achieved a thick stack of swatches . . . no, a drawerful . . . no, boxes and boxes full. And I imagined taking out my boxes of swatches, of an evening, and riffling through them the way some people browse for hours, lost in reverie among the pages of old photo albums.

4.

A Visit to Los Feliz, and
All Around L.A.

During a summertime trip to Los Angeles and San Francisco to visit friends, I quickly discovered that California, like New York, was infected with the knitting virus. Some of the most enthusiastic knitters I met there were members of a group called the Church of Craft, a three-city organization that seeks to "find moments of creation in all our lives." Before I left home, I contacted Allison Dalton, the "reverend" of the L.A. branch, and told her I was coming to town. She in her turn e-mailed all her flock, telling them I was looking to interview knitters. Six of them responded, and from those six, who wrote to me asking, "Are you going to visit Edith's shop?" or "Have you heard about the Knit Café that's opening up?" I was put in touch with a total of eighteen knitters in California and another five outside the state, who in turn led to other knitters, and so on and on, lengthening my path and causing it to wind through regions I had not anticipated.

In addition to her initial help rounding up subjects, Allison was generous in another way: She offered to let me meet the Church of Crafters at her place in Los Feliz. When I arrived at the apartment—which was filled with books and yarn and fabric and all manner of creative clutter—Hilda Erb, several months very nonchalantly pregnant with what she calls "The Extra Kid" and dressed in overalls, was already curled up on the couch, working away on a sweater for her six-year-old daughter, Robin. Allison was copying Japanese embroidery patterns from an ancient tome onto sheets of graph paper. Then came Stephanie Rogerson, who had never been to a Church of Craft meeting and had never met Allison or Hilda or any of the other Crafters, but who'd been somehow included in Allison's e-mailing and had turned up, with plenty to say, after writing to me by way of introduction: "I am thirty-four and have been a knitter for a long time. Oddly, I've never gotten any better, but I keep doing it." Talk about knitting started with no prompting from me and continued pretty much unabated, without and then with Shannita Williams-Alleyne, who arrived late, all apologies, after being stuck in infamous L.A. traffic.

Church of Craft, Los Angeles

No other form of "Dainty Work" is so conducive to sociability and a general feeling of bonhomme as a piece of knitting. . . . It occupies the fingers, yet leaves the mind free for "idle converse all the while."

—ADDIE E. HERON, *DAINTY WORK FOR PLEASURE AND PROFIT*, 1894

HILDA ERB: I bought all this white wool and didn't know what to do with it. Then I read something on getcrafty.com [see pg. 261] about dying with Kool-Aid, and I thought, *I'll try that.* So I tie-dyed it. [She holds up a neat square of mottled-pink stockinette that smells strongly, sweetly, like cotton candy.] This is going to be a sweater, scarf, purse, and hat—a little set.

I've been knitting since I was eleven, back in the '70s, and there were all these great books that came out back then about handicrafts. I remember being fourteen years old and wanting to make all these things my grandmother couldn't teach me, so I used *Make It with Mademoiselle.*

STEPH ROGERSON: I went through a hat phase. I called the hats *kiptiques:* half *kipahs,* the Jewish skullcaps, and half *toques,* the Canadian mass-produced knit winter hats. That one year, everybody got a kiptique. Basically, I knitted them all fucked up and I did alternative dying with this crappy yarn I'd found. I tried curry, which made everybody sneeze; onion skin, which had a nice tea effect; and beets, which made the yarn look dirty. I think the hats were really successful, because they didn't make any sense: putting craft and nonsense together.

HILDA: You buy these things, and they all look perfect—*perfect*. And I think, *That's why I like to do these things—because they look homemade.*

STEPH: I've tried cutting up stuff I've made and then patching it together and sewing it. That wasn't very successful. I was hoping for it to unravel, but it unraveled in an unruly way. I thought I could control it, but it was a disaster.

HILDA: That whole idea of unraveling pieces of clothing—that's so artistic. You learn how things can be twisted and turned. I've made some things where I combined thin thread with bulky thread on the same needle using garter stitch, and the effect is exciting to me.

STEPH: You sound like you have the ability and the skill and the background to try things and also be kind of productive. I feel a lot less productive, because I only know two things: I know how to knit and I know how to purl. And I know how to start it and I know how to end it. I'm not as free and able. I still want to make pretty things, and when they're not pretty, I feel unsuccessful. To be free and let things screw up is a little bit hard. My mom taught me how to knit, but she never taught me technique. That was up to me. I think I was about ten years old, making these really tight things, and everything was dirty because of my sweating hands. So ugly! [The women laugh.] I remember being so proud, like, "Oh, wow, look what I've done!"

I have this really great cotton/wool yarn I got in Johannesburg a couple years ago. These women had spun it and dyed it, and there's something post-apartheid about it: women's work, black women's work.

It seemed so loaded that I had a cry about it. I bought this wool 'cause it's so powerful, but what if I screw it up? I want to do something there's no way I can screw up. So I thought, *Maybe I should do an afghan.* I've been waiting for two years to feel like screwing up isn't an issue.

HILDA: I buy a lot of thrifted yarn; I can't bring myself to buy a little ball for $8. Thrifted yarn is a good way to just dive in and work through things, to experiment.

STEPH: Generally, when I start something, I have some kind of idea, like I wanna make a whole bunch of scarves that look like worms. That's what I focus on for a month and a half. And then that feels successful because I've completed the plan. I don't feel free enough to just knit and see what happens, because I feel like I'm wasting not just the material but my time. My mother's approach to it is, "Just go!" But I say, "You can't just drop me off on the freeway and say, 'Find your way.'" I'd like to try a sweater, something really basic, nothing fancy, as a way to understand patterns, as a way to get less arty about it, more concrete. Then maybe I'll feel freer about being arty. I'm not there with knitting yet. I'm totally closeted. I hide when I do it, maybe because I'm not very good, so why tell everyone? In fact, I told my roommates I was coming here today. And they were like, "You're being so weird about it. Are you in a porn ring? What's happening?" And I was like, "No, it's about knitting." And they said, "You're a knitter?" Yes, I'm out of the closet, I'm a knitter. I guess I have a weird relationship with knitting, I'm discovering the more I talk. For me, it's always been about being solitary. I guess the Church of Craft meetings are just the thing.

ALLISON DALTON: The meeting really worked out well last night. This Asian girl walked in to the coffee shop, and she was kind of uncomfortable. She was fidgety and didn't know where to sit, she didn't know what to order, and then she moved over to a couch separate from our two tables, so there was no way to have a conversation with her. But by the end of the night she and these two other women were sitting at a table, having an amazing conversation about film and art and high school and being an artist, and she seemed so happy and comfortable. There's some heavy stuff that goes on for me when I'm watching people.

You don't get a lot of community in L.A. This is mostly women getting together and doing women's work, and it reminds me of everybody sitting around, making a quilt together, doing those things that used to be part of a social ritual—a religious group, because it was usually a religious group that was the center of a community. There's something about coming together and creating around other people who are creating: People learn stuff or they don't; they dig through the boxes of things I bring or they don't; they talk or they don't—it's different every time. I always thought that I was a very unspiritual person and not into those ideas of connection and communication and community. But I watch it happen every single time we have a meeting. There's not a whole lot that's good to believe about religion, as far as I'm concerned, but when you write off religion, which most people I know my age have, you don't have that community anymore.

HILDA: If I sit down in a café and start to knit, people will come up to me and talk.

ALLISON: We had so many people come up to us last night. It's amazing how many people are interested. And the thing about knitting is that everybody gets it—nobody approaches it in any sort of ironic way.

[Shannita comes in with a breathless hello, sits cross-legged on the floor, and takes a baby sweater she's working on out of a "Stitch 'n' Bitch" bag (see pg. 97), one in a series that Hilda made out of old tablecloths.]

SHANNITA WILLIAMS-ALLEYNE: I have five or six knitting projects going at a given time.

STEPH: I would say that about pretty much my whole life—there's a minimum of ten projects going on. I used to get stressed out about finishing, but I don't now. Stuff gets finished. Maybe it'll take thirty years; some things only take four days. If it doesn't get done, that's OK, too; something else takes its place.

HILDA: I have a reputation for finishing. My friends come to me and say, "Finish mine."

SHANNITA: I've only been knitting for five months. I've been crocheting since I was ten years old. It took a while for me to grasp the whole idea of knitting because I'm left-handed. My grandma taught me how to crochet by looking in the mirror. Then she said, "Perhaps that'll work for you to knit." It didn't work; I didn't get it; I didn't understand it. Then I found all this really cool yarn at a shop, and I crocheted with it and it looked awful. So I said, "OK, that was a waste of time." I went to the lady at the yarn shop, and she said, "Well, I don't know why this is so difficult for you, because you use both hands when you knit anyway." A light went on. I bought a book and I taught myself how to knit. Now I don't pick up my crochet hook to do anything but finish.

HILDA: Even though crocheting is so fast, there's something about knitting that just appeals to me.

SHANNITA: The fabric is much nicer. There's a different quality to the yarns, especially the fuzzy yarns. You can't use good yarn to crochet.

HILDA: Crochet makes crappy yarn look good.

SHANNITA: When I crocheted, I was the resident baby-present maker. I did baby *anything.* Then I made afghans. Everybody I know has an afghan. But I have friends now who see me knitting and they say, "Can you make me a sweater?" No, I can't make you anything. I have to make something for *me.*

STEPH: No wonder you like knitting more!

SHANNITA: It's a lot more comforting. It gives me a chance to mellow out, because I have to think about what I'm doing. If you're upset or annoyed or going through something, you can take your frustration out on what you're doing. Sometimes you get something beautiful, because you were in a meditative mood; sometimes you make something really ugly, because you had to get it out. I don't want to put anger and aggression and negative energy into anything I'm making for someone—I firmly believe that you can do that, and I don't want to give that to a baby. So I've got this one piece, this horrible scrap; I like to say I'm "practicing" stitches on it. . . .

HILDA: I can go for years without picking up my needles. I ran across these beautiful vintage rayon yarns, and that got me knitting again.

STEPH: I'll go for years without knitting or sewing. But there's always something being made, whether I'm not knitting, but I'm taking photographs; or I'm not taking photographs, but I'm drawing; or I'm not drawing, but I'm making cowboy shirts. Now I'm looking at these balls of yarn from South Africa, asking myself, *God, will I ever make something with them?* But when I'm in the knitting phase, then it's constant, like smoking: After dinner is the perfect time to smoke, the perfect time to knit—with cocktails. When you're in the zone, there's never a bad time to be knitting.

HILDA: I play chess with my daughter. She's got this Flintstones chess set and she's learning how to play. It's the perfect time to take out my needles. An hour and a half of saying, "No, you can't do that" is sort of tedious.

SHANNITA: I started out as a pattern whore. My grandmother decided that I was going to clean out her closet, and the reward for that was all her old knitting patterns. Now I've got all these awesome patterns and I think, *What am I going to do with them?* It's easier to use patterns because I haven't mastered design yet, although I want to. But it's hard because I'm not a small woman. I can't wear 90 percent of the patterns I like.

ALLISON: Nothing's classic anymore with patterns; they're ruffly or Southwestern. . . .

STEPH: Or they go up to here. [She moves her hands up under her breasts.] Why do I want a sweater that I'm hanging out of?

HILDA: Two years before I met Mark [Hilda's husband], I was a single mother working in a law firm, working from 7 A.M. to 7 P.M. and not being able to see my daughter, just coming home and sleeping. The hardest part of that was being brain-dead, not having the energy to create anything. It's come back since I stopped working there.

SHANNITA: If I'm not creative, I'm stifled; I'm blocked.

STEPH: Dissecting knitting is making me think about intent and motivation. I'd like to make a black sweater, because a black sweater would make me feel pretty, and that would be nice to give myself. And it goes with everything, and it'll take me forever to do, and by that time it'll be winter again. Also, I could learn to do a pattern. There's no pressure; it's just something to do while I watch VH1's *Behind the Music.*

SHANNITA: I want to make a living being creative, not having to punch a clock or be in a corporate, structured place. I've become completely obsessed with knitting—I know there's a way to make money with it. It might change my relationship to it. That's what happened to my writing; once I got paid for it, having to chase down the money drove me crazy. I have a different relationship with the knitting so far. I like it a lot, it's fun, I'm good at it. You shouldn't live to work—work should enhance you.

I've met the most wonderful knitters. I'm coming back from Canada, we're going through customs at the airport, there's this woman talking about how she's upset because she couldn't bring her knitting needles on the plane. *Knitting needles? What?* We start talking. Turns out, she has a website and sells yarn. She's a retired television writer who's in her seventies, and she's having a great time. I've met so many magnanimous people, and they're so giving. You say, "I'm having a problem with something," and they're like, "Oh, I'll help you." I've never met people like that before, ever.

An extraordinarily busy (and stylish) mother of two, small e-biz owner (Mamarama, which sells hip, handmade clothing for mothers, mothers-to-be, and babies), and founder of the L.A. Stitch 'n' Bitch, which holds biweekly get-togethers, Vickie Howell was nevertheless brimming with new plans on the afternoon we met in Santa Monica. The latest: to start a nonprofit organization to a donate high-quality, used maternity clothes to teenage programs—which she told me all about in a rapid-fire monologue. Needless to say, for the first few moments of our encounter, she struck me as intense.

Soon enough, though, as we began to talk about knitting, Vickie showed a more relaxed side. The atmosphere was conducive to ease: We sat in the dim, deserted back room of a coffee shop as the afternoon sun edged in around the solitary window, and a waiter on roller skates, with nothing better to do, glided slowly around the empty tables.

VICKIE HOWELL

[Knitting] needed to be born
again—born of a new genera-
tion, one content to love it as
a means of personal expression.
Knitting for knitting's sake.

—MARY THOMAS, *MARY THOMAS'S*

KNITTING BOOK, 1938 (1972)

I'm 100 percent a feminist. That said, I think that we as feminists have done ourselves a bit of an injustice. We were fighting, so we let our relationships with our sisters become blockaded by what we needed to do: climbing and pushing and taking. We've gotten away from something core that existed in the knitting circles, in the sewing circles and quilting bees, in the big-kitchen cooking, which was women working together in a nonthreatening atmosphere, really talking to one another in a place where there was no competition or any need to put up a front. I feel fortunate to live in a time when I believe that we can bring this all full circle, because I think women have a gift for communicating and being creative. It affects every aspect of our lives. To be able to knit and yet still be able to produce movies or write stories or raise children or work for the stock market—I think it's brought balance back to a tipping scale.

I worked in a corporate atmosphere for a long time, at International Creative Management (ICM), as a producer's assistant. I turned my nose up at knitting because I was used to stereotypical, kitschy-looking socks made with cheesy yarns. It wasn't until I walked into this room at Edith Eig's yarn shop, La Knitterie Parisienne, [see pg. 103]—and I think a lot of younger people say this: You expect it to be a room full of eighty-year-old grandmothers knitting socks for their grandchildren—and I was wedged between a casting agent, a mom, a movie producer, a grand-mother, and a twelve-year-old girl, and I was surrounded by these amaz-ing, high-end yarns, that a whole new knitting world opened up for me.

My mom always knitted and crocheted; we were a crafty bunch. She tried to teach me how to knit years and years ago, and I just wasn't in-terested at the time. A friend of mine who's a casting agent had been go-ing to Edith's, and literally for a year she was trying to get me to go with her. I thought it was kind of interesting but that it would be just another project I'd have to do; it didn't sound that appealing to me. Finally one day—I was pregnant then and feeling like I wanted to do something for the baby—I went down to the shop and I just got hooked, and I have not been without a project since.

Edith's people are very loyal. You go there and it's always packed, and you can say, "I'd like to learn how to knit," and she'll ask, "What do you want to do?" I happened to have a picture of a hat with me, and she said, "OK, this is the kind of yarn you need," and she handed me a pair of needles and taught me how to cast on and check the gauge. As long as you get your yarn there, you can come back as many times as you want, and she'll walk you through the process.

I would go to Edith's on Saturdays with my girlfriend, and I did that for a while because I was working on sweaters. I'd get to a stopping point, and I needed help. Nine times out of ten, what would happen was I would see something else—a yarn I wanted to work with or a project someone else was working on—and I'd start a new project of my own. Then I was on bed rest for my pregnancy, so I couldn't go to Edith's at all. *Ahhhh!* It was terrible. So I started doing easy things, things I could give as gifts that I didn't need help with or that my mom could help me with if I dropped a stitch.

Since I've had the baby, I've been back there a couple times, but it's hard because it's forty-five minutes away. That's one of the reasons I wanted to start my Stitch 'n' Bitch group—my friends aren't necessarily crafty, and geographically, it's hard to find community in L.A. It's not like New York. L.A. County is about sixty miles wide; everybody has to drive at least half an hour to get to these meetings. We don't walk anywhere in L.A., so where are you going to meet one another? Community has to be created here.

My company was mentioned in *Bust* magazine as a place to get cool baby clothes. I was flipping through it, and in the back was an ad for Stitch 'n' Bitch in Chicago. I e-mailed the hostess: "Is there an L.A. group?" and she said "No, it's up for grabs, you just have to create your own logo." I wanted to hang out with other hip women who were interested in knitting but who also wanted to talk about social events or recipes or anything. It's interesting the people who responded. I thought because of its name that it would appeal to all these funky, hip girls, but not so much. I was really surprised. We get a wide array of people, but it's cool because these aren't necessarily people I would have struck up a conversation with in the first place. Knitting is sort of our common thread.

I see things all the time that I'd like to make. I'd really like to make some cool bags with wooden handles. I'd like to make a funky coat. Knitting is a hobby, it's my relaxation. I'd like to not have to meet deadlines with my knitting, because I tend to be very structured in a lot of ways—that's the Scorpio side of me. I have a lot of agendas, and I really find that I need something creative for myself that doesn't require any expectation of me. With knitting, I've been able to relax.

I also crochet, but I don't enjoy it nearly as much. I also sew. I find that I have all these other projects going on that I sort of dread. I've noticed that I seem to tire of other crafts. Knitting is the one thing that steadily, for nine months, I don't go without a project, whereas if I'm decoupaging or making a pair of pants or a blanket, I'm done. Still, it doesn't appeal to me to have my life fully centered on knitting or any one thing. For me, knitting has helped me find a sense of balance, which is something that, being a career woman and putting it on hold to raise children . . . well, it's important to find other things that make me who I am, so I'm not only Tanner and Tristan's mom.

Knitting has a rhythm, and that's why I'm drawn to it. You don't have to know the complexities of it to make something that's decent that you would wear. I pretty much use only stockinette and garter, and I've gone crazy a few times and done a little seed stitch here and there. I was flipping through some magazine the other day, and I saw this great '40s-style suit; the jacket was really fitted with a belt, and it had these rhinestone buttons, and the stitch was something I didn't know. I'd be interested in learning that new stitch just for the jacket.

I'm just starting to make things for me to wear. I'm doing a poncho kind of thing; for some reason, I'm into orange all of a sudden. I like to give gifts, though, and people are so appreciative when you give them something you've made, because no one does that anymore. Also, you can make something that would cost a lot more money if you bought it. Plus, I'm really huge on keepsakes. I think that's something we've lost, having things to pass on to our children.

I pride myself on being a very crafty gal, but when I didn't have knitting down in the first ten (or thirty, or 420) minutes that I tried it, I felt frustrated. (Ironically, I think this is one of the reasons I haven't grown tired of it yet.) But once you get into it, especially if you're working with the right materials, it really sort of puts you into a meditative state. For me, I have a little problem relaxing. I don't do well just sitting—I think that's one of the reasons you get a lot of Hollywood types doing this. I worked with so many people for so long who were high-strung because of the fast pace of the industry; you almost don't know how to relax—you always feel like you have to have something to show for yourself.

I was going to be a producer; I was very driven. I worked in a business that was male dominated, and being in a male-dominated place, you get these ideas about cooking, motherhood, knitting—anything that has to do with the old-fashioned ideal of being a woman; your shackles go up when you hear about things like that. I think that some women closet knit because you have this inner battle and you say, "I am not going to be anything that any oppressive male has ever had in his mind that I will be. But I really like to knit." Or "I really like to cook." Or "I really like to garden." I think a lot of women are smothering this instead of embracing the fact that we have the opportunity to have both. Being creative is inherent. I've been lucky to have the opportunity to create that life for myself.

Of all the people who asked me, "You *are* going to talk to Edith, aren't you?" Vickie was the most persuasive. She didn't just ask, she offered to meet me at Edith Eig's shop, La Knitterie Parisienne, and make all the necessary introductions. "Actually," she said, "it'll be a good excuse for me; I haven't been able to go in months."

As it happened, I arrived before Vickie (stuck in that always-infuriating L.A. traffic). I walked into Edith's wide-front, near-Hollywood shop and found . . . Hollywood. Producers, actresses, and assorted industry women sat crowded at a table, surrounded by what seemed like mounds and mounds of yarn that tumbled, literally, from everywhere. The women looked up when I entered the room and gave me a thorough up-and-down, then went back to their knitting and loud gossip. Edith was easy to pick out of the group. Paris-elegant with her coiffed blond hair and a perfect pedicure poking through her sandals, she was laughing and gossiping with the best of them in her thickly accented English.

While Edith took care of a few matters of business, I walked around the enormous shop. Yes, there were scads of yarn—of every conceivable kind and color, on shelves, in baskets, behind locked glass panels, pouring out of shipping boxes—12,000 line items in yarn alone. But there were also books, magazines, special needles and gadgets, samples of Edith's assorted blanket designs, and an enormous loose-leaf binder filled with clips about the shop. I flipped through the articles. "Knitting is like comfort food," Edith had quipped to *Canada Fashion* a few months earlier; and to *Foxnews.com* she mused that her shop was "like a psychiatrist's office." In nearly every article, she was referred to as the "knitting guru to the stars."

In the two hours I spent in the shop, Edith paced around taking phone calls, sniping with Merrill—her ironic, white-haired, East-Coaster husband who works the register, does the inventory, and largely runs the place—checking in on the group of knitters in the second room, sending one of her two assistants to help a woman who was just learning how to knit, greeting customers, taking a moment to expound on some troubling topic (a shop down the street had just stolen her latest pancho design and was selling the completed garments for $300), showing me a new arrival of $75/skein cashmere, and throwing me a *bon mot* or two, all the while knitting with fine red kid mohair on #1 needles, making a gift for the new baby of her friend, actress Julianne Moore. Vickie, flustered from the traffic, finally dashed in wearing Edith's pancho design, which she had double-crocheted herself with some difficulty. Edith walked her back through it, explaining it quickly but expertly, not giving up until she was sure Vickie understood what had gone wrong.

Through all the hullabaloo, Edith either walked and knit, with her ball of yarn tucked under her arm and the phone sandwiched between her head and shoulder, or stood and knit, with the ball resting on a countertop. The ball was constantly falling to the floor and she didn't miss a beat as she stooped to pick it up. She'd completed some twenty-five very neat rows by the time I left.

EDITH EIG

... [Le tricot] devient un art véritable dans l'execution de certaines dentelles. ... Ensuite de ce double caractère pratique et artistique.

... [Knitting] becomes a true art in the making of certain laces. ... And so it has a character both practical and artistic.

—*LE TRICOT*, 1923

I'd been in the knitting business for twenty-six years, six of them in Los Angeles, when we moved from Parsipanny, New Jersey, to be closer to our three children, who all work in the "industry." We have 5,500 customers, including those who do mail order. Right now, I'm about to shoot the pilot for a TV series that will air on the Home & Garden Television channel; I'm not sure, but maybe it will be called *Stitches of Style*. It will have do-it-yourself projects, starting at the beginner level, and I will interview people and probably have celebrity guests.

I've been knitting since I was five. I learned how to do it in school in France; everyone learned that way then. After school, I didn't start knitting again till I was in my twenties—I didn't even knit for the kids. Luckily, I had family in Paris who sent very good things. I worked on Wall

Street and didn't want to go back to it after the kids were born, so I opened my first store, The Canvas Pad, which was originally just for embroidery, and little by little I started knitting again.

Knitting is a relaxing form of entertainment. And it's a very creative field. You can put in knitting whatever you want—style, color—and you can make it in your size. At my shop in New Jersey, I had a lady who was so big that I had to use two tape measures and have help measuring her. Knitting was rewarding for her—she could make things that fit her.

You need a lot of philosophy to knit. Philosophy is an approach to life; so is knitting, because you're creating something. When people knit, you can recognize them by their style, the design and the color they choose. I can tell when a person comes into the store which yarn they will pick up, which color yarn describes them. It reflects their personality. I had celebrities contribute squares to a blanket for charity, to benefit the families of police and firemen who died on September 11. I can tell without looking it up which square was done by which celebrity.

I remember all the names of my customers. It's nice to know when you come into a place that somebody knows you. Knitters will travel—they'll always choose where they want to go. I've always been successful because I don't charge for teaching; if you buy your yarn here, learning to knit is free. You just have to encourage people. It's a good addiction—it's legal, nonfattening. Also, you have to know your yarn. You have to study it; you have to know what it will do. We had a young girl who came in and wanted to learn to knit on cashmere. I wouldn't sell it to her. She said, "But I can afford it!" I sold her a $5.95 ball of yarn. It's enough to learn on.

Ellen Margulies, one of the first women to respond to Vickie's Stitch 'n' Bitch postings, told me about her own link to Edith and La Knitterie Parisienne: "My mom, who still lives in Brooklyn, came to visit me a while ago. She'd heard of La Knitterie Parisienne, so I took her there. My mom was talking with Edith, and after a few minutes of conversation, they found out they'd lived just a few blocks from each other before Edith moved from New Jersey out to California. Edith took so much time with my mother—she was making a sweater for me, and Edith helped pick out the colors and textures I liked, and then she had my mother knit up a gauge. We sat at this table, talking with these other women, and it was something I had never experienced before. And my mother had this great story to tell when she got back home."

Ellen brought a bagful of scarves to the coffee shop in Santa Monica where we met one late, breezy afternoon. She was so visibly excited to have made these scarves—to have found yarns that pleased her and to have picked the various combinations—and to have the chance to show them off. She pulled them out, all stitched simply of eyelash yarn and ribbon—in dark olive and Fizz (green and white and pink plumes, like chrysanthemum fireworks); black with tiny red pompoms; and sheer burgundy with burgundy tufts—and ran her hand over their cushiony surfaces. Then, one by one, she tossed them exuberantly around her neck and let out a wide grin, a woman in love with her creations.

ELLEN MARGULIES

The invalid who finds time hanging heavily on her hands, and wants some light occupation that will not tax her feeble strength . . . turn[s] to knitting . . . with positive delight.

—*The Self-Instructor in Silk Knitting, Crocheting and Embroidery,* 1884

About a year ago, I had three disks removed and replaced in my neck. The surgery was really great in that when I woke up I felt the difference, but the recovery was awful. I had to wear a hard collar for three months. I couldn't knit when I was in the collar, because I wasn't allowed to turn my head, and I had to wear it twenty-four hours a day. It was very intense. I couldn't speak, and I couldn't swallow. I was really freaked out about not being able to talk, because the doctors said it would only last a week but it just went on and on. I thought I was just going to be speaking in a whisper for the rest of my life. And then one day it came back, like that.

The weird thing was, after the collar came off and my voice came back, I had this burst of creativity in knitting, and I haven't stopped since. I had been knitting a little bit before I got hurt, because I just wanted to get the skill back. I said, "I'm going to start small," so I started knitting baby hats and donating them to the children's charity Stitches from the Heart. And then I said, "Now that I'm getting a little more experienced, I want to do something bigger." So I made a blanket and donated it. I had started a blanket before the surgery. I saw it sitting there in the bag and thought, *Why don't I finish it?* So I finished it. And then I was reading an article in *Vogue Knitting* about this yarn store in Vermont that was donating proceeds to breast cancer research from a scarf made with eyelash and ribbon. I bought the kit, made it, and loved it, so I thought, *I'm going to try to find different combinations of this and make my own.* A friend of mine opened a store here in Santa Monica, and I walked in wearing this black scarf with tiny orange balls knitted through it, and she said, "We have to sell this in the store!" I said, "You're kidding. I was just sitting watching TV doing it." She said, "I want you to make six." So I made six and they sold right away. Then I made another half-dozen with burgundy ribbon and matching eyelash, and they all sold, too.

When I was recuperating, I met this incredible bunch of people online, because I spent so much time in front of my computer. There's a whole community of women called the knit bloggers. We all have blogs online, and we talk about our knitting. I read the blog of one of the women I met, Beth, every day. I started e-mailing her, and we got friendly, and she said, "I'm going to teach you how to knit socks." I said, "Socks? That sounds a little intimidating." But then I said, "OK, I'll give it a shot." So she sent me the materials and posted the first group of instructions on her blog, and I took a picture of the completed socks with my digital camera and e-mailed it to her, and then she put it up on her blog. Then all the other bloggers got inspired to make socks, too.

A funny sideline is that my husband, who's in advertising, was going on a shoot in Vancouver. I wasn't working then—I was on disability—so I went with him. Beth lives in Seattle and she had some time off, and she said, "I've always wanted to go to Vancouver; it's not that far." She drove up with her husband and son and met us in Vancouver. I brought my socks with me to show her. We had never even spoken on the phone. But the minute she walked in the door, it was like we had known each other forever, and now we're friends for life. She's pregnant and due in November, so I'm going to throw her a virtual shower with all the knit bloggers. Everyone's going to knit her something and send it to me; I'll send it to Beth, and then we'll go into a Yahoo chat room while she's opening her presents.

I think people are really into cocooning now, and knitting feels like a comfortable home kind of craft to do. It's much less solitary than it used to be. When I went to the first Stitch 'n' Bitch meeting, I was sitting with all these women, and it was amazing to me. Most of us weren't very experienced, but it was all about bringing people together. Also, I love that you can be a pretty beginner knitter, and just with a few stitches, you can have a variety of textures. I love that now there are all these novelty yarns, like eyelash or two different yarns twisted together.

I've never taken an art class before, but these days I'm looking at things differently. I have a notebook and a digital camera and I take notes and pictures of color combinations and textures, because I feel as though I want to try designing instead of following other people's patterns. I bought some yarns from Japan on eBay, and they had funny names like "mascara" and "fascinating happy yarn." Being surrounded by all these colored yarns when I was recovering, it might sound hokey, but it just made me happy. I got this plastic bin, and I know I bought way too much yarn, which a lot of knitters tend to do. I would open the box and look at this stuff, and it just made me so happy.

Knitting saved me—I don't know what I would have done without it. There wasn't that much I could do when I was recovering: I couldn't work; I couldn't read. I was really getting bored of TV; how many episodes of *Trading Spaces* can you watch? I dreamed about knitting. I would dream that *this* was what I was going to do today, or I'd dream about some project I wanted to do in the future. It just became part of my life. My daughter was at school; my husband was at work; I was by myself. I would sit out on the balcony in the sun and feel the ocean breeze, and it was the best thing. It saved me, because I was being creative. I'm starting to become an artist, and I really like that side of me that I never even knew was there before.

I t was early evening in Santa Monica when I left Ellen. The sky was turning rosy and soft as the day wound down, and suddenly the notion of getting back in the car, heading into rush-hour traffic, seemed like the worst and most claustrophobic of ideas. Instead, I decided to head a few blocks closer to the ocean and look for a fiber arts shop, Wildfiber, that Ellen had told me about.

I found it easily enough—a tidy storefront on a tree-shaded block. It was practically deserted; the shop had opened up that day (a Monday) only for a special class, and it was by virtue of pure luck that I had found the doors unlocked. Bending over a basket of lusciously soft handspun, hand-dyed yarn from North Carolina, I stood and turned smack into the store owner, Mel, a New Zealander who moved to California seventeen years ago. She's been knitting for forty years, she told me, and as I was to discover, she had plenty to say on the subject.

MEL CLARKE

There is something in every human soul which seeks to create a thing of beauty.

—BARBARA WALKER, *A TREASURY OF KNITTING PATTERNS*, 1968 (1998)

My mother was an avid knitter, and my childhood was full of comforting handknit cardigans and pullovers, which I would wear with great pride. She taught me one evening when I was eight years old; I vividly remember being tucked up in my parents' double bed, under the eiderdown, feeling the sense of safety that knitting has given me ever since. I don't recall if it was my idea, but I loved it from the start. I didn't ask my mother for much help, although I remember my first Peggy squares being full of mistakes.*

*Wondering what a "Peggy square" is? So did I. Information about it came to me via Clara Parkes, the editor of *Knitter's Review* (see pg. 60) who sent me a link that explained that it was named for Peggy Huse, a New Zealand girl who, in 1930, at the age of four, was seen by a popular radio hostess, knitting little squares. It occurred to the hostess that other New Zealand children could be induced to knit squares that would later be put together to make blankets, and she broadcast her idea over the airwaves. "Peggy squares" subsequently became a big hit throughout New Zealand.

I taught my daughter, India, to knit two years ago when she was fifteen, although so far it hasn't become a compulsion or obsession with her the way it is with me. She doesn't neglect her schoolwork for knitting, as I did, and she hasn't yet learned to knit while she talks on the phone (the sign of a true addict). My heritage is Scottish and English, and in New Zealand the influence of wool is unavoidable. The smell of wool, fresh off the sheep's back at the county fair shearing competition, is as much a part of my childhood memories as cotton candy.

I have been knitting pretty consistently since I first learned, with perhaps the occasional two-year hiatus (new babies and feeble attempts to start alternative hobbies, such as needlepoint, were the main reasons for the gaps in my knitting history). During my thirties, I wanted mainly to work with color knitting, either Fair Isle or intarsia, and I started making my own designs and patterns. This was a big breakthrough, to be able to make my own designs. Before that I worked mainly from patterns, with the emphasis on stitch patterns. Making my own designs turned out to be very satisfying, and I began to plan more and more complex intarsia designs for my children and for myself.

Wildfiber already existed when I took it over at the end of 2000, but not so much as a knitting store—it specialized more in surface design. I have brought in a large selection of yarns, and the emphasis now is much more on knitting, since that's what I know best. I love teaching, for several reasons: It's satisfying to introduce others to this craft that I love so much; I meet delightful people and have made many new friends; and I learn such a lot from teaching, about human nature and also about knitting. New knitters sometimes have a completely different and original slant on it. You know how it is when someone doesn't know the rules, so they don't worry about breaking them? Most of us have been taught to knit in a certain era or place, or by a certain type of knitter, and have developed habits accordingly. New knitters have no habits or expectations, so they come up with ideas that are quite unique. For example, there was a woman in one of my classes who loved all the fun, textured yarns but was less interested in knitting techniques—increases, decreases, how to measure gauge. She started making rectangles and squares out of exotic yarns, all kinds of crazy color schemes. Then one day, for fun, I wrapped one around my wrist, remarking what a cute cuff it would make, trying to encourage her to do something with the odd-shaped and eccentric bunch of swatches she was assembling. It gave her the idea to make bracelets, which she's been doing ever since. I've even bought a couple from her. Let's face it, I can't knit everything.

There is such a marvelous selection of exotic and beautiful yarns these days, and since I have a yarn store, I'm constantly thinking of new projects and seeing yarns I want to experiment with. That can be confusing, and I have to limit myself. Sometimes I follow an existing pattern from a book or magazine, but again, I get the most enjoyment from making up my own. I often start with knitter's graph paper, especially if I'm making up an intarsia pattern. The biggest challenge about making up a pattern is that it's a risk; it doesn't always turn out to my liking. Sometimes I simply start knitting and make it up as I go along. I try to write the pattern down as I go, but I'm not always conscientious about that, much to my regret later on when someone asks me for it.

It's a challenge to try to get more free and creative with my knitting, and of course there's always another stitch pattern to experiment with. As much as I learn from knitting each project, there's always more to learn. I try to be as happy as I can be with each project I'm working on, stay in the present, and not focus too much on what I don't yet know or haven't yet mastered. I try to encourage new knitters to stay in the moment and enjoy each project as it unfolds.

I get most of my inspiration from things I see, whether they're in books, in nature, or in other crafts. There are so many things to be inspired by, and most of them have nothing to do with knitting. I once did a series of designs—brightly colored, mostly on black backgrounds—inspired by the work of Clarice Cliff, an English ceramics designer from the Art Deco period. I'd bought some pieces of hers, inexpensively, at yard sales and thrift shops in New Zealand, and loved the way she used color and shapes—very stylized and abstract florals and landscapes.

I love to knit alone or in a group—it doesn't really matter, just as long as I'm knitting. When I'm knitting alone, usually in my home, it's a meditative pastime, calming and therapeutic, even though my mind can be abuzz with thoughts. I also knit with a group once a week, and that is an entirely different pleasure. The conversation in the group is always interesting, even controversial. Sometimes it's about knitting, but mostly it's about life.

I love to knit so much that I don't usually need to set aside time; I just find myself doing it, whether it's early in the morning, in the kitchen before anyone else in my house is up and about, or while I'm watching a movie in the evening. I try to knit regularly, because that's the way to get things finished. If I let a project languish for too long, it's harder to go back and pick it up.

I am just a knitter, pure and simple. I knit because I enjoy it and I love to make things. Just the act of knitting, the repetitive motion, is a pleasure for me. I've knitted many things, from complex color patterns to simple little baby booties, thigh-high socks (when I was a teenager and wore miniskirts) to a striped vest for a biker in the movie *Fear and Loathing in Las Vegas*. I've never fixated on one particular thing to knit. I just enjoy being creative.

My mother, Daphne, is the best knitter I know. She lives in New Zealand, and the women there are incredible knitters. She will tackle anything and experiments a lot. Her knitting is very even, and her colorwork is exquisitely tidy on the inside (a daunting task when there are hundreds of ends to weave in). She is what I would call an intrepid knitter. Those are the best. Years ago, she knitted a simple, natural wool pullover for my dad. He loved it and wore it until she had to patch the elbows. She would complain about him wearing it so often when she'd made him other, newer sweaters, but it was his favorite. When he passed away three years ago, I was touched to see that she had him laid out in that well-loved sweater, even though for years she'd complained about him wearing it.

In many ways, knitting has been the theme of my life. Always a hobby bordering on obsession, it became my livelihood when I started designing my own handknits and having them made by women in New Zealand, to sell here in the United States. After a few years of that, I started selling designs to companies such as L.L.Bean, and Pavo Real in Boston. The years when I was designing a lot were probably the ones when I knit the least. Anything I would dream up could be knitted quickly by someone else, so I had less incentive to knit myself. I must have forgotten momentarily how much pleasure I get from the simple act of holding the needles.

The Addiction Deepens

All manner of magical creations dawn and appear
from the birthless sky. . . .

—PADMASAMBHAVA, *YANG DAG GI GZANG 'GREL CHEN MO*

Before I ever left for California, I went back to Linda's shop for more of Jamie Harmon's vegetable-dyed merino/angora. (I'm not the only person addicted to this yarn, I would later discover; a lot of Linda's regulars have found themselves hopelessly drawn to the stuff, and they all rhapsodize some project they've used it for.) The supply had changed since the last time I'd visited, and after my initial disappointment, I reasoned that I should move on to something new anyway. I inched my way around the shelves, touching my fingers to the skeins. The shades of yarn I found myself most lured by were rich and jewellike or slightly exotic, a hair's breadth away from true "blue" or "red"; none of them were colors I would ever use to make into garments for myself. But this fact added a dimension of practicality to my plan to swatch. The more I thought about it, the more it made sense; I could work with colors I loved but did not feel compelled to wear, and I could buy one skein at a time, an arrangement at once indulgent and affordable.

Time to move on, but I could not keep my hands off the Jamie Harmon yarn. The new assortment of colors was brighter and deeper than the previous batch. Yes, it was time to move on, from the sea green of my last purchase to . . . more green. Two hues caught my eye. The first was like the springtime, overnight bloom of tree buds—vivid, almost chartreuse—with a whisper of the more mature green that will emerge in the coming weeks. The second was a hunter's green that looked as if it had been set to soak in ocean water, then left to bleach in the sun. I picked these over shades of dusty blue and ember red and persimmon, and the moment I had absolutely decided on them, like a psychic, Linda emerged from the back room to ring up my purchase. I half-expected her to ask me what I planned to do with only these two mismatched skeins. Should I admit that I was swatching? Should I lie and tell her I was

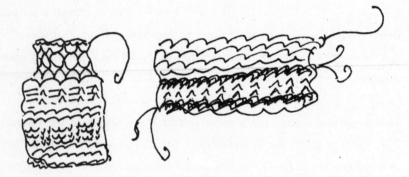

making pom-poms for hats, or booties for my cat, or dresses for the dolls of the little girl—my favorite neighbor—in the building next door? But the only thing Linda asked me was: "Do you want me to roll these into balls for you?" And I was filled with the reassuring sensation that Linda would understand not just swatching, but anything else I could come up with.

Back at home, I noodled around for a while with the bright green yarn, making pretend lace and sloppy stitches of my own "invention" till

I was fed up with the resulting hodgepodge. Then I tried a couple color changes, just for practice, picking up the darker yarn for a stripe or two. Ho-hum. I'd begun to flip through the Barbara Walker treasury, searching for patterns with comprehensible instructions. I hit upon smocking, a sort of honeycomb pattern that called for a multiple of only eight stitches and eight rows. The pattern was largely a matter of knitting and purling. To create the bind that effectively pulled two columns of ribbing toward each other to create the honeycomb effect, the instructions

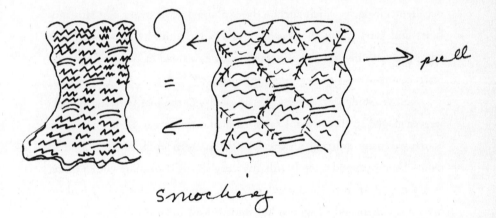

smocking

read: "[D]raw loop from between 6th and 7th sts . . . and knit it together with the 1st st . . ." I couldn't quite envision this action, but when it actually came time to execute it, I found that with needles and yarn in hand, translating word into deed was pretty simply done.

The finished splotch of smocking, though, was not terrifically interesting. About two inches square (I realized too late that I should have doubled or tripled the suggested stitch multiple), the swatch, when it lay flat on a table, showed practically no character whatsoever. I had to hold it in both hands and pull it taut to reveal its patterned insides.

Next up: Palm-Tree Puff. Taking a lesson from the smocking, I cast on twenty-four stitches instead of the bare-minimum suggested multiple of ten-plus-four. This pattern was of alternating lines of puffs—shaped like the spades printed on a deck of cards—strung together with narrow trunks. It was twenty rows long, and its instructions called for yo's, and the initially puzzling ssk's and p2 tog-b's. But the Walker book had an excellent glossary, which succinctly explained yarn overs and slip-slip-knits and purl 2 together-backs, and again I found that when I was equipped with my needles and yarn—*doing,* instead of just *reading*—the instructions proved not at all complicated.

And yet somehow, despite the simplicity of the instructions, the pattern managed to throw me. I sat with it one warm, early evening in my courtyard—my knitting on my lap, the pattern book on the table in front of me propped open beside my very slowly dwindling vodka tonic, as my dog, desperate for a game of catch, repeatedly dropped a ball on my foot. I managed to ignore her and to knit up several rows. Then a sinking realization: Something was off—I had an extra stitch at the end of the seventh row. I thought: *It's fine; I just miscounted,* and I decided to just knit up the stitch. But then I had another extra stitch at the end of the eighth row, and two extra stitches at the end of the ninth. I counted up the stitches of my swatch, then the stitches in the book, factoring in the increases. Way off. I couldn't tell where I'd gone wrong—hadn't yet figured out how to tell my knit stitch from my purl—so as my husband

and a friend arrived in the courtyard to play a game of chess, I began to unravel.

Palm Tree Puffs

In the ensuing half-hour, things went from bad to worse. I started knitting the Palm-Tree Puff again and found that I was off by row five. I wondered if I'd misread the instructions for ssk, so I went back to the glossary but discovered no error. I unraveled the swatch again. Again I cast on twenty-four stitches and managed to go twelve rows before I found myself with too few stitches on the needle. All the while, the two courtyard chess players (and one would-be ball chaser) chattered and laughed (and spit a ball out at my foot) while I tried to ignore them. "Gee, that's too bad," one of them said, as I unraveled my stitches again. "Is it our fault?" I glowered and gave a sarcastic smile but said nothing. I cast on one more time. "This is it," I chided myself, ready to be through with the ordeal. I polished off my drink for fortitude, sat up straight, and as I knit, I began to count out every stitch, every row, muttering them under my breath. And this time, on my fourth try, two hours from when I'd started, I finally managed to pull off a perfect rectangle of four Palm-Tree Puffs, looking for all the world like the springtime tree buds that the color of the yarn had first suggested to me. "Look! I did it!" I shrieked to everyone in the courtyard, delighted with my accomplishment. Everyone (I like to imagine even the dog) had to admit: It was a beautiful little thing.

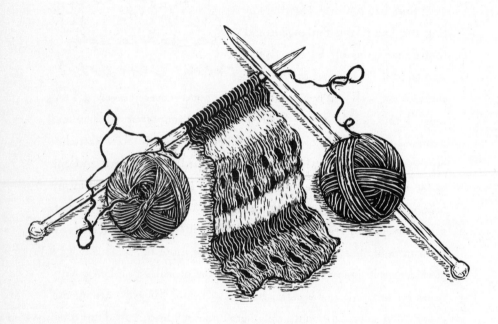

5 .

Bob's Donuts and Beyond

Nancy Lenehan is another member of the Church of Craft who came to me through Allison Dalton. An actress, she was auditioning the afternoon I met with the Crafters at Allison's apartment, and couldn't join us. "How about Friday morning at the Farmers Market?" she suggested. "It's one of the few places we have here that is distinctive, and we might stumble upon some older knitters (like bird-watching)."

We arranged to rendezvous in one of the market's enclosed, open-roofed pavilions—imagine sitting in a sunken patio or at the bottom of an empty swimming pool with a wood-slatted deck encircling above you—at Bob's Donuts, an L.A. institution. I found Nancy and her seven-year-old daughter, Adeline, sitting at a table under an umbrella, looking bright-eyed and cheerful. Right after introductions, Nancy presented me with a gift, a circular Clover yarn cutter, while Adeline, freckled and shy, quietly set to work on a piece of embroidery.

As Nancy had prophesied, the place soon began to fill up with lady knitters, retirees in groups of two and four who strategically took over tables nearest to the exits and coffee stands, settling into their seats like hens on a nest and pulling needles and yarn from bulging shopping bags. One of them, Sue Micich, a jolly-faced tower of a woman, approached our table with her sleepy-looking friend, Viva. They greeted Nancy, oohed and aahed over Adeline's embroidery—a girl in a bonnet, shaping up nicely—then began talking about their latest knitting projects. They talked for ten minutes straight, hardly pausing for a breath, then gave us a wave and headed off to commandeer a table of their own.

NANCY LENEHAN AND ADELINE, SUE MICICH AND VIVA

Today knitting can still fill odd moments. Think of all the frustrating periods of time we spend just waiting: waiting for the coffee to boil; waiting in the car; waiting until the fish bite; waiting until someone else's favorite program is over so we can switch channels; we all have our own particular waits. Those who rode to work could finish a sock in a week if they would spend the time knitting. Imagine!

—ELIZABETH ZIMMERMAN, *KNITTING WITHOUT TEARS*, 1971 (1995)

NANCY LENEHAN: I knit in five-minute increments all during the day—it's probably annoying to everyone around me—and I could knit in the car, even if I was driving, if I had to stop at a lot of long red lights.

I'm an actor, so I work on sets; as soon as the director says "Cut!" every-one's knitting hats. The show I'm working on now, even the lighting people are doing it—men, too. You see this sharing that goes on: "What are you making? Where'd you get the yarn?" It was big on the *Ally McBeal* set, the *Felicity* set, the *Judging Amy* set. Knitting's not just for the little old lady in the corner anymore.

I've been doing it since I was a girl. I was always fascinated with nee-dles and thread and various yarns. I taught myself with books. They say it skips a generation; my mother didn't knit or sew or anything, but it was a sweet, sweet thing that she did—she always allowed me to buy this stuff: sewing machines to make clothing, needles, and yarn, and she would encourage it. Now I see Adeline, and I'm thinking, *Is she gonna want to do it, too?* I don't complain or push, though; I don't want to do that to her.

A lot of people try to learn and they go "*Ahhhh!* I can't do that!" but I had a good experience. I like doing jigsaw puzzles and crossword puz-zles; I like putting things together. There's just part of my brain that likes to do that, and knitting's the same way. It's problem solving. I have always done it, and I've always wanted to do it. I know that when I first started knitting, I was holding my breath—I wanted to really get it. I was working on these Fair Isle patterns with different colors wrapped around different fingers, and I'd be holding my breath and constantly holding them up to look at them. Knitting wasn't immediately comfortable, but obviously, I pushed through, because I wanted it so much. But I think it's relaxing, now. It gives you focus: back and forth, back and forth.

I don't sit for hours at a time and knit. I tend to weave it in around other things. I like to try to visualize the pattern as I'm reading it. Part of that is experience: I can read a pattern and see if there's something that's not going to work, like the arm is too long or the sleeve is too tight. I don't like graphing, but I do like to sit and read. I can't *not* knit. I love it and have to do it, and if Adeline won't wear the sweaters I make, I'll make sweaters for [Los Angles-based charity] Stitches from the Heart, which donates them to kids in hospitals. I have no patience to knit a sweater for a grown-up——never have, even with the big, bulky needles and the big, bulky yarn.

Finishing is a problem for me. If someone were to tell me, "We're going to lock you up in your house for thirty years," I would think, *That's fine, I have plenty to do*. I'm always starting more things than I'm finishing——I'm always a little underwater. I very often find things in thrift stores that someone didn't finish from the 1930s, and I realize that maybe she never got to that, maybe she hated it, maybe she ran out of time, maybe she's like me. Maybe when I'm gone, my unfinished things will give someone pleasure to finish. I read once that there were process people and progress people——some people want to get it done in one afternoon and some people enjoy the process, and I think I'm more of a process person. I could just start things forever and enjoy that. But I have to have someone give me permission not to finish it; I think it's wasteful not to get it out. I tend to want to make something to keep someone warm. I'm not so much interested in knitting something you can hang on the wall.

Once I got a family going, it became really difficult for me to hang out with my girlfriends, so knitting became the guarantee that I could do that——making sweaters and eating cookies. My needle arts group has been meeting every Thursday for nine years; the community is so much of it. I like to keep track of people. I love the camaraderie.

Hello, Sue! [Sue comes over and hulks benignly over the table. She takes out a tiny hat in soft, speckled cotton yarn.]

SUE MICICH: I make blankets and hats for Stitches from the Heart. Other people, they do little sweaters. This is my friend Viva. This is a washcloth pattern. [She tugs the thing out of her bag.] It's about thirty-three inches square, on the bias. When I get tired, then I start down again. This way, you can use up your scraps. I'm making this one a fuzzy one—you just try all different things.

I was five years old when I learned to knit. My mother taught me. My grandma, my great-grandma—we all do it. I don't crochet, I only knit. I've got nothing but time. I don't know how many hats I've made— I wish I had kept track. I quit doing them for a while and only made blankets. But I used to do fifteen hats in a week.

There were twenty of us in Stitches from the Heart to begin with. Now there must be 2,000 of us. You can do anything: You can sew; one lady makes burial gowns, because a lot of preemies don't make it. We have another lady who crochets toys. The hospitals go on the Internet and say, "We need blankets" or whatever. It's all free, all volunteer, all charity. You'd be surprised by how much time people put into these things—they're beautiful, no schlocky yarns, good quality. Before I started knitting for the hospitals, I knit afghans, large ones. I gave them all away.

Knitting's a craft that's been lost for a long time. It used to look bad, used to look junky—not sewn together right, one arm longer than the other, neck too tight. Now there are beautiful yarns. This yarn for the little hats, this came from England. I like to work on pretty colors. Now they have so many beautiful styles—they come out with great patterns in the knitting books and magazines. It's all coming back, especially the Irish fishermen sweaters. I just finished a scarf with an Aran pattern; it went to Israel to a friend's mother. As my knitting comes off the needles, people ask, "Can I have that?"

 S omeone told me today that this woman is opening a knitters' café," Nancy, feeding me potential interviewees from across the country, wrote to me before I left New York for California. It would be, she said, "a place to knit and chat, with always a teacher on hand to help you untie some knots. Interested?" I said I was, not then really knowing if I was—not really sure what was meant, exactly, by a "knit café." But then Suzan Mischer, the owner of the Knit Café, contacted me—thanks again to Nancy—and invited me to have a look at her soon-to-open shop and hear about its inception and philosophy.

I arrived on a crystal-clear holiday afternoon; the whole neighborhood surrounding the café, sandwiched on Melrose Avenue among high-end antiques shops, was deserted of cars (and, since this was L.A., after all, pedestrians). The indeterminate movement of two women behind the café's plate-glass window was the only thing stirring, it seemed, for miles. I entered to find one of the women—Suzan, as it turned out—sitting at a long table, inspecting great heaps of yarn. Another young woman, Suzan's assistant, Tina Marrin, was sitting cross-legged on the floor, embroidering the letters "KC" onto the backs of mustard-colored chairs with orange thread.

The place was airy and light and decidedly swank. The walls were painted shades of blue and salmon, and the floors were being prepped for marbleizing (also in blue), then a tossing with red and pale blue carpets. There was yarn everywhere: on the giant table that took up the whole center of the room, on nearby chairs, in baskets and in bags on a coffee table near the windows and in the back room. Suzan, it was obvious, was a woman having a field day with yarn, with decorating, with realizing, bit by bit, her vision for what she calls "just a comfortable place for me to hang out with my girlfriends." She walked me around the room, waving her hands happily at the empty walls to show where her yarn shelves would hang. "I'm thinking of spelling out 'Knit Café' in yarn, or I could make stripes." Talking about the possibilities made her smile widely with satisfaction. Excitedly, she began to dig things, like high-heeled, knee-high boots with knitted uppers designed and made by Tina, out of boxes to show me. She had two weeks to go until opening. She clearly couldn't wait.

Knit Café

A genuine love of the beautiful is innate in the heart of every girl and woman.

—Mrs. Sibbald and Helen Grey Souter,

Dainty Work for Busy Fingers, 1915

Suzan Mischer: I worked at CBS for twelve years, as vice president of specials and documentaries, and I had a wonderful career. Then I had a son. And after two years of schlepping my son all around while doing shows, I just decided it was too much work and not much fun for him, so I stopped working and stayed home. From then on, I had to learn how to stay home and not have a secretary and not get dressed up. I did a million things: I worked for charities; I had another kid. But what I really did was knit all the time.

Last August, I got the idea for the café, because I think there are a lot of women around who are like me; they've changed their careers and they want to be with their kids, but they also want to do something that feels good and feels creative. Whether they stay home, or go to the park, or wait outside school for their kids, they can take knitting with them. And they can knit here. Knitting's portable; you can pick it up and put it down; there's an ease factor to it. Women whose grandmothers made complicated sweaters are seeing these incredible yarns and getting excited about them and realizing, "I can make a scarf." They see that they can pick up needles and do something snazzy.

I learned to knit when I was seven; I learned from my grandma. She was one of those remarkable grandmas who was from a different school of knitting, where they just tore it out and tore it out and tore it out until everything was absolutely beautifully perfect. She was an incredible knitter, and I still wear a lot of her sweaters—that's how well-made they were, and now they are actually in style again. I come from her sensibility, although I don't follow through on the detail work like she did. But I still have more of a traditional approach than this generation or younger has.

I think younger girls, like Tina, are really into the renegade quality of knitting. I talk to so many girls who get totally charged up by slicing it and dicing it and breaking all the rules. And that's not anything I would have done with this beautiful yarn; it would never have occurred to me. Tina just told me she had this yarn and she was drawing in Magic Marker all over it. These girls are finding a real place for a different kind of personal expression. I'm not sure if that's because of where we live or the times we live in, but they bring a different point of view to knitting that I find so exciting. And I hope the café will attract them, too, not just the moms.

TINA MARRIN: Back to what you were saying about "personal expression": When people see that I'm making art with my knitting, they say, "Oh, you're making some sort of feminist statement," but I'm just making something I think is cool, that has texture I can't get with paint or anything else. Yarn is just another medium. People like me are drawn to it, and we tweak it because we don't have that baggage where someone's told us we have to carry the yarn this way or that we can't twist it that way; we're ignorant of that.

SUZAN: You make up your own rules.

TINA: That's true, and I think it's the same with other people my age. I taught a knitting class for some friends. They kept getting their balls all tangled up, so they lined up the yarn and ran it through the sewing machine and made scarves out of it. Big wound-up balls—they just didn't want to untangle them, and what they did with it was very cool. Originally, I learned to knit because I was going to Cal Arts, and a friend of mine there was learning. She just wanted someone to come with her. I got totally into it. I just blew off everything and knitted like crazy. Like Suzan says, you get into a rhythm, and it's great when that happens. What I was doing in art school was knitting ski caps and I thought, *What do I do for my senior thesis show? Do I show a pile of ski caps?* And I figured, *This is what I'm addicted to doing; I'm drawn to these things.* So I threw them all together, a pile of ski caps and some other stuff: two rugs I had hooked; a limp, elaborate yellow cutout from an enlarged Xerox of Dolly Parton's hair; ten hand-painted fingernails with Brian Ferry portraits on them.

SUZAN: I knit bags, scarves, sweaters, turtlenecks, things for my kids— I don't do anything experimental like Tina does, like sewing a scarf onto a sweater or taking a thing and turning it upside down or backward. Tina has an artistic point of view, whereas I'm more of a person who just likes to knit. Tina comes at it as a painter comes at a canvas. More and more I see it as an artistic outlet, but I use my creativity for the colors I choose, or the buttons I choose, or the ribbons. That's how I see the difference. Tina makes one-of-a-kind things that hang in galleries.

I don't see anything I make ever being in a gallery or even necessarily being sold. An artist thinks of things differently—wants something to be on display, wants something to be seen, thinks of it in terms of how the fibers are working. A lot of people in L.A. are really into fiber arts; that's a whole different education. Maybe I'm selling myself short, but I don't think so. I think that the choices I'm making for my shop, and the designers I'm bringing in, are really good formats for my own creative expression. From the colors I pick to the merchandise, this environment is definitely my creative vision.

TINA: I think a big part of my creative vision has to do with mistakes. For me, a mistake is a learning thing, after which I say, "I have to remember that the yarn was too heavy for that." I don't ever rip it out. I use it: cover it up, or stitch over it, or incorporate it; maybe I like the way the mistake looks. What would happen if I did that even more? I did this circular knit sweater, because I like knitting without seams, and the top part was way too tight. That was a mistake, so when I decided to give it some room under the arms, I let all the stitches fall. Then I put a panel behind it with all these strings, and that turned out to be a great mistake—I would never have come up with that technique otherwise.

I went to a knitting convention a while ago, where I met the Twisted Sisters (see page 223). They were having me explain to people who had been knitting for twenty or thirty years how to do things, and I'd be like, "You just knit it, and then you turn it sideways—that's it." Knit when you want, purl when you want. I will never rip out. If I made a sock and it was way too big, I'd turn it into a hat. And that's the other thing—if I knit something and it's the most hideous thing, I'm going to wear it. I spent all this time on it and money on the yarn. I'd cut it up or felt it; I would never undo stitches.

SUZAN: I'm so much lazier than that. I have oodles of things that I just loved making, but I never finished them. I have sweaters that I love every part of, but I don't have them stitched together. They're held together with safety pins.

TINA: Wear them with safety pins!

SUZAN: [Laughing, then turning reflective] It's been seven years since I stopped working at CBS. For a long time, I felt like I sold out. At some point, you come to a place where you move at a different speed, and you start to find things that fulfill you—that's when I started carrying my knitting around. As I started carrying my knitting around, there was a whole group of women that approached me. I think there's a safety valve in knitting where, if I like to knit and you knit, it's OK for you to talk to me—I'm a nice person, probably a friendly person. I think that one of the things we look for is a way in which we can connect, even if we're sitting in the same room without talking.

I was carrying my knitting around, and I was very aware of people. They would come up to me and ask, "What are you knitting?" In the same way, they would also come up to me when I was pregnant and ask, "Can I touch your tummy?" There was just something about the tradition of knitting, the calmingness of it, the nurturing aura around it that invited that response. It's part of what I think happens when knitters walk into a store and talk to people they wouldn't normally say "Boo" to.

I don't know if that's spiritual, or cosmic, or just a comfort factor that we're all looking for that comes from a place deep down in our hearts where we can say, "This is what's safe for me." Instead of showing us our differences, knitting tends to bring us together.

Tina spent the whole summer after we met knitting boots—like the ones Suzan had shown me at the café—"like crazy. I'm thinking I will make a stock boot out of lopi yarn and get a pattern down on one type of highish heel," she wrote me at the end of August. As for Suzan (who reported a surprisingly busy summer season), she had, with tremendous anticipation at the time of our meeting, been planning to carry garments and kits by several knitwear designers. Teva Durham was one of them, and Knit Café was set to stock her California Mommy-Daughter ponchos, short capelets knit in the round with cotton tape yarn.

A Manhattan native and new mother, Teva started designing sweaters and scarves just a few short years ago and now has her own website, loop-d-loop.com, through which she showcases and sells them. On the day we got together in the paint-spattered back garden of her mother's SoHo painting school, Teva had just come from a meeting at *Vogue Knitting*, where she'd presented her trend report for the next issue—sketches accompanied by info on the latest stylings, trimmings, yarns, stitches, motifs, and colors. Her giant four-month-old daughter, Olivia, was with her, pedaling her chubby legs as she dangled from her mother's chest in her carrier.

TEVA DURHAM

We crochet and knit in the first place because we wish to produce something of our "very own" doing. The creative instinct is born with us, and the skill to fashion pretty and useful things from little material is denied to few.

—*KNITTING AND CROCHET*, 1915

I love the idea of seeing the body as a whole, of seeing your side as being integral. We're not a front and a back, we're all the way around. I'm just fascinated by the circle and by knitting in the round and how meditative that is—the idea that you can take one string and never break it and create a shape that'll fit the body. Somewhere along the line, I started to see the body as a series of tubes: the arm is a tube, the leg is a tube, the head is a tube, the torso's a tube, and I try to design things that are basically tubes with a little shaping. My T-shirt, for example, is one continuous strand from the neck down. It has some shaping: you bind off at the neck and the armhole, and you cast on under it. You go out a little for the sleeve, and you basically end up with a spiral.

I teach knitting in the round to people who've never knit before, and I find that it's easier for them than the traditional way, because they don't have to think about the wrong side of the fabric and the right side of the fabric and knit and purl—they can just knit. The shaping part they seem to get if you draw a circle and put in the different segments; they can see how the increases line up. People who've never knit before are finishing garments. You would never think of a T-shirt as a first project, but it can be. I've always had this broiling in the back of my head, even when I was studying writing, how a story is a circle: You have a beginning and middle and an end, but it's like a snake with the head biting the tail. I love the concept of not seeing things so linearly.

My grandmother taught me to knit when I was really little, but I never finished more than a few inches of a scarf. She was really a great knitter, and I do think it was sitting in me, that it was sort of hereditary. She used to knit really bizarre things. Everything was oversize and in wild colors; she used to make these big capes, and she would actually wear them. Often, she would use the big, fat needles, which is something that I do, and she would knit several strands of yarn together. I have a few things that she made. She loved loops, and I have this big coat that has loopy fringe all over it.

When I was in high school, one of my nicknames from my mother's friends was "Seventy Sweaters," because I used to go to the $1 bin on Canal Street and get all the interesting sweaters. My mother made me a canvas holder that hung on the wall: It was nine feet by nine feet and had three-foot pockets; each pocket would hold several sweaters, so I had this soft sculpture to hold them all. When my mother's artist friends came over to drink Café Bustello, it was looming there on the wall. I wasn't knitting then, I was just admiring all the sweaters in the vintage shop.

Later, when I lived in London, I had a friend who knit. She was knitting, and I thought, *Maybe I should do something.* I passed by a Patricia Roberts yarn shop, and I saw a complicated sweater in the window and bought the kit. It was way, way beyond my capability. It had a chart with basket-weave stitch and colors; the woman in the shop told me I couldn't do it. I said, "Just show me what this chart means." She said, "You read right to left on the right side rows, and left to right on the wrong side rows; if it's a dot, it's a purl." It took me an hour to get one row done. I didn't know how to tie on the different colors, so it had holes in it. But I did manage to finish it—it took me six months. It became like a crossword puzzle, and that's what I love; I love symbol craft. It's like new math. It's a funny lingo, and I enjoy that. When I write patterns, I have to write in that lingo. It can give you a headache. It's like deciphering a code.

I wasn't teaching that much before Olivia was born, but that's been exciting. I find that certain people pick it up like that; once they get going, they just have to keep going. Some of my students come back to class the next week and they've hardly got anything; some come back and they've got a scarf and a hat—they stayed up all night. I teach now at The Open Center [a "holistic learning" center]. I proposed it to them; they were looking for some art classes and they asked my mother if she wanted to teach drawing from the right side of the brain. She said she wasn't interested but, "Oh, my daughter teaches knitting." So I sent a proposal and I tried to emphasize the spiritual aspect. I thought, *Here's my opportunity to teach knitting in the round from the get-go.* In a normal yarn shop, I teach on straight needles, and I think it's a lot to digest: learning how to cast on, knit, and purl all in one night. This way, I have my students cast on to a sixteen-inch circular needle, and they go around and around and make a tube, and then they bring in their tube the next week and I show them decreasing, and then everyone has a hat.

Knitting is almost like an itch you have to scratch. For me it's kind of a manic thing, good for bipolars. It's like smoking. I can't sit in front of the TV without knitting. Actually, I just got rid of my TV, and now I listen to books on tape, because I was spending a fortune on videos. Since I knit for magazines, I knit for hours and hours and hours, and I'd rent three videos a night. But the books on tape last for twelve hours. I love that, because I'm getting literature at the same time. When I look at a piece now, I remember which book I was listening to when I made it.

Just today I realized that when I was starting to work for *Vogue Knitting* and starting to design, I had no idea of what my personal style was. I used to love the designer Nora Gaughan, and every time I'd see her new sweater, I'd know *she* did it—she uses these beautiful, intricate cables. A while back, I had turned in a sweater to *Interweave Knits*, sort of a Renaissance tunic with a frilly collar. It's modern at the same time as ancient. Melanie Falick, *Knits'* editor, called me to say she loved it, and what she loved about it was that she could tell it was mine without looking at my name; it had my signature style. And I said, "I've got a signature style?" That was a milestone.

Now I can say, "Now I can die." Is that terrible? This comes from having parents who are artists—from an early age, I felt that I had to achieve some monumental thing. I was always trying to find my own little niche, not as a painter but something at which I could be a success. I realized at some point that it was kind of unhealthy to want that kind of attention from acting. But even after I'd made knitting my career, I still believed that if you want to make a living, you have to make a name, and to do that you have to be ambitious. At least now I try to couch it in creating something positive and sharing. It's not a prima-donna thing—you can't trademark what you make, and it's hard to compete with the overseas market, and the magazine work can be grueling, too. You can spend forty hours making a sweater; then you have to type the pattern and size it. It's two to three weeks of work for each sweater, and you get paid between $500 and $700. I do love it, but there's something a little sick about it. It never fails that the yarn comes late and I'm knitting before the deadline; it's like giving birth. It's like you're pushed to the limit, and your fingers are cramping. I try to see how many inches I'm getting per hour and how many more hours I still have to knit. But I always get the sweater off to the post office at the last minute—the collar takes longer or I decide to redo something. After I'm finished, though, it's elation, as though I've just come through a marathon. Maybe I'm addicted to pain. Maybe that's why I don't mind that my business hasn't made any money yet—because it's made me joy.

I feel great that I'm really *doing* this, that my pieces are coming out the way I wanted, that I'm figuring out what it is that's special about me. I have a different way of working with knitting in the round, and I'm coming up with new ways of making a garment and making it very shaped to the body. My things are fresh and young. They hint at costume and nostalgia. Some of them are inspired by *The Little Prince*. I love aviator things, and Renaissance things, and medieval things, but not so they look corny; I want them to have an element of drama.

I think that if you make something with your hands, you can't be all that bad, and the world is a better place. There's that philosophy that says the energy of your hands will live in the object; if it's made by hand rather than by machine in a country where people are being exploited, that positive energy goes out into the world. It's a constructive, positive force, like gardening. It's like making your own little organic vegetable garden.

Knitting is something you take a long time to get better at. It's a discipline; things come out wrong, and you have to figure out why. But it's also like playing an instrument. If you're someone who's following the pattern with the same yarns that are published in the magazine, that's like playing a symphony—it's imitative art. There are people who will substitute different yarn and add their own little touches, and people who make up their own patterns. Other people can't figure out how to change the pattern to fit their bodies. When I teach people, I try to loosen them up. A lot of students are afraid they've made a mistake, and they'll obsess about it. They won't like this one little loose stitch down there in the corner. I'll say, "Oh, that's all right, it's handmade." From teaching, I've gotten to see how people work with their hands, and everybody's hands are different.

My mother was raised Catholic, and my father was a little confused; we were brought up very agnostic, and we were never brought to church, although my grandmother told me about God when I was little, and I envied people who went to church or thought there was a god. So I was always searching. I wanted to believe in something, but my parents didn't believe in anything except art. My religion was art, and in my family, the artist is revered. I was always searching for some connection, and what I found was that art is something that can be a religion, but in a way, I like craft better, because it's so much more concrete. It gives me some grounding. Some people see fashion as frivolous, but to me it is very deep to clothe yourself or to create something for the human body with your hands and a piece of yarn: There was nothing and now there's something. When I was growing up, we never got ceremony, because we never went to church. But it was ceremony when I proposed the Renaissance tunic to *Knits* and when I did the drawing and I said, "Here's the design I'd like to submit." From the conception to buying the yarn and then actually making it live—it's taken me ten years to do this, to design something and have it come out looking like the drawing and for me to be happy with it. It's like my ceremonial robe.

Editors of magazines, even of knitting magazines, are a beleaguered bunch: besieged by phone calls, harried by deadlines and endless strings of meetings, always straddling the line between order and complete chaos. Trisha Malcolm is no exception, perhaps in part because she is the editor of not one, but two magazines: *Family Circle Easy Knitting* and that grande dame of knitting publications, *Vogue Knitting*. I called her early one day to arrange an interview and she granted me one, almost within seconds—no time to dally or have a nice chat, even at 8:30 in the morning.

On a brutally humid July afternoon, I took the subway down to the magazines' SoHo loft offices. I emerged from the station to find the sky heavy with ominous storm clouds; by the time I'd made it up to Trisha's desk, dark sheets of rain were beating against the windows. It was a cozy scene for talking about knitting—like finding yourself nestled, in autumn, into a chair by the fire or sitting near the waft of warm dinner smells on a snowy night. There, in Trisha's snug office, we were surrounded by dozens of yarn samples in skeins and balls and cones, and everywhere there were photos and sketches of beautiful sweaters, and books and magazines piled high on the floor. And outside—no immediate concern of ours—the weather raged.

TRISHA MALCOLM

[Y]ou are actually knitting up human history. With your needles and wool you are retelling ancient tales and forgotten legends that are part of every man's birthright and heritage.

—JAMES NORBURY,

KNITTING IS AN ADVENTURE, 1958

Never in my wildest dreams did I think I would have a job in knitting. I used to be a school teacher in Australia, then I started backpacking around the world, and then I came to the United States. By accident, I ended up in a job at *McCall's* magazine, and I didn't even work in the knitting department. A couple years later, I took a job at *Vogue Knitting* in an editorial position, then I moved on to some sewing projects at Butterick. When this job came up, I was in the right place at the right time. I didn't want the job—I was sewing and not knitting, and I never thought I was experienced enough; I never thought this could possibly be my job. You know how you're so in awe of something? I love to look at *Vogue* and *Elle,* and my favorite magazine is British *Vogue*—I get so excited when it comes. And as with any magazine that you love, when you're not involved with it you look at it and each page seems to be a special thing. That's how it was for me with *Vogue Knitting.*

My biggest memory from an issue of *Vogue Knitting* is the Donna Karan tree sweater. This, to me, is the greatest sweater ever. It's really gorgeous. I knit it, and I actually found the one mistake in the chart and had to fix it. I was going through a divorce at the time, and I was just crazy. Look at these charts! [She pulls the magazine down from the shelf behind her desk and opens it up to the dog-eared tree sweater pages.] I knit like a mad person—it was very therapeutic. I had never come across anything that was such a knitting challenge, such an exciting thing to knit as this. Everyone else I know who knit it felt the same way. I think five of us in the office knit it at the same time. As well as taking the clouds out of the pattern because I'm short, I went to a smaller needle size, and I knitted it in different yarn—gray, with a wool/mohair blend. Other people's sweaters were different lengths; some had clouds, some didn't; everyone's had a different color. There's a whole chart of things that I'd never seen before. It was a knitting experience, and it's very rare to come across something like that.

Every magazine has certain processes, and it was very interesting for me to see what went into making a magazine like this. An issue begins with trends. If you look over there, you'll see we get a lot of European publications. And once a year, I get the joy of going to Pitti Filati, which is a yarn show in Florence. We see a lot of stuff there, take a lot of photos, walk around the stores. It gives you a definite sense of the trends as they emerge. We have a Trend Report that we send out to our designers—Teva writes this [see pg. 135]—and that's to inspire them to do designs for the upcoming season. We react to trends, and we definitely react to the fashion world in terms of what's going on in knitting. We write information and articles, but I really believe that people buy our magazine because they want to knit the sweaters.

We get the trend stuff, and then the designers send us swatches and sketches. Here's a Debby Bliss sketch, and a swatch [she digs a square of mauvey pink with a small ruffle out from the pile on her desk; the sketch is of a cardigan edged with the ruffle]. We've chosen our yarn—which is this baby cashmerino, a wool and cashmere and microfiber blend. From there, we come up with what we're going to put in the magazine, so it becomes sketches, like on this storyboard, and that turns into a story. And, of course, everything in the magazine is hand-knit.

We work with a lot of different designers, and we try to present some cutting-edge new yarns. For instance, we're working on the winter issue right now, and there's a trend for fur, so we've got some fur yarns. Sometimes we use more traditional yarns that are long-lasting. Something like 95 percent of our readers keep every issue of *Vogue Knitting*, so you need some longevity to the yarn—you want them to be around for some years to come. People see a yarn in a sweater we publish and 70 percent, 80 percent of them say, "I want to knit it in that yarn, that color." They're not interested in any other yarn, any other color.

Some of our readers are experimentalists—there's definitely an element that is very creative at heart. There are some people who would never knit a sweater from our magazine, but they take elements from many sweaters and create their own. They say, "This sweater has an incredible collar; I want to take that collar and put it on another sweater." People find things that they like or that are interesting to them; there might be a new cast-on technique they've never tried before, and they'll say, "Oh, next time I'm going to try that."

We get the design solutions in from our designers, and we select from them—as wide a variety as possible. From there, we go to photography, and then the sweaters come in with their instructions and we double-check them. Obviously, there are mistakes every now and again. We do what we can not to have them, but it's part of the deal. We get slammed for them, and we get slammed because we're *Vogue Knitting*. But every knitting magazine has mistakes; every knitting book has mistakes. It's not possible to do a knitting publication and not have a mistake.

I can't answer "Why knit?" as an individual anymore, because I've gone way beyond that. I have to say, working around yarn is just a lovely, lovely thing to do. At any time during the day I can pick this up and stick it through my fingers, you know? It's terribly indulgent to work here, but I have to tell you, I haven't knit a stitch in I don't know how long. It's the middle of summer; I have a child, so I don't get time to knit at home; and if I'm in the office, I don't have time to knit here. It's awful. Being around all this yarn, I get so excited; I think, *I have to swatch something, try this out.*

Knitting is something my mother taught me and something her mother taught her, and it's primarily a female thing—and I mean that without being sexist in any way. The thing I love about it is the connectedness of women. I love that this is something that people have been doing for generations and generations, and that I'm working toward this activity continuing, because I think it has a huge amount of value. At some point in the past, everyone made their own clothes; some people have never considered that everything was once handmade. To be able to make one thing for yourself is an incredible accomplishment and an incredible feeling. Knitting is very earthy, and I'm not talking about granola and Birkenstocks. I'm knitting with this yarn that comes from a sheep, and it's spun the same way that wool's been spun forever. It's a connection with the earth and with real life. I think that's a big thing for us now in our society; we want to connect with the planet.

I think this magazine feeds the knitting engine. It connects people. Whether you live in New York City or you live in the middle of Iowa, a sweater may speak to you and make you want to knit. We really do try to have a variety of sweaters in every issue. We try to open ourselves up. Sometimes we put things in we don't necessarily like, thinking, *You know what? There's someone who's going to love this.* And nine times out of ten, there is. Young knitters are a big problem, and that's something we're working on addressing right now. There's definitely a need in that market, and it's a need that wasn't there four or five years ago. The thing about a magazine like ours is that we can put thirty to forty patterns in every issue, but not every issue is going to speak to every reader. But in each issue, there are things happening like this [she picks up the latest issue of the magazine]: this is a great, long jacket, slightly tailored, with a loopy fringe around it. And we'll get a lot of complaints about this skirt from readers: "Who can wear that?" [She's referring to a picture of a white flapper-style skirt, fringed all over, that ran first in *Vogue* before being featured as a pattern in *Vogue Knitting*.] The people who ask that might be isolated from a younger, hipper audience.

I've been in this job for five years, and I've learned a lot of things about knitting that I had no idea of. I learn more every day. Every now and then I see a new technique, or I see something done in an unusual way, or I see a design that's a great way of doing something. For instance, this is a ruffle [she waves the Debby Bliss swatch again], but it has an eyelet in it. Three years ago I had never seen a ruffle like that; why *not* put an eyelet in there? Knitting is always surprising. It's never boring. It's fluid; it's organic, but it's also so personal; it's an extension of you. What you choose to knit—and you're also choosing your yarn, you're choosing your style, you're choosing your color—is a very personal expression of where you are *right now*. Something you knit three years ago you would not knit now—you'll knit something totally different. It's not just your experience, it's a direct reflection of yourself.

Knitting feeds our creativity; it's our self-expression. The thing about self-expression in knitting is that it's based on technique, so you have to have a certain repertoire of techniques in order to express yourself. Some people spend their lives building up their techniques, building up their stitch library. Some people are dedicated to color work; some people will only knit cables; some people will only knit stockinette. It's random, but that's the thing about it—you can find something that appeals to you.

Thank God I get to see knitting every day. I do miss doing it. But I feel that with what I do, at least I'm creating vicariously. And when I do knit, I *knit*—usually sweaters. Right now I've got this cute blue one on the needles for my son; he'll probably be grown out of it by the time it's done, but I refuse to have guilt, ever. You just do what you can do.

"Who can I pass you on to?" Trisha mused as I sat with her in her office after our interview, jumping into the whole spirit of the telephone-like game of the knitting path, where one knitter leads to another. It only took a moment for the idea of Catherine Lowe to dawn on her. "You've never seen anything like her before," she said.

As luck would have it, Catherine, a former member of the comparative literature department at Williams College (among others), who still comports herself with the proper, measured poise of a university professor, was visiting Manhattan one sweltering day in July. She'd driven down from her upstate New York house to shop for fabric for her Couture Knitting Workshop, and to see what was what—and new—in the world of fashion. We met in a sleepy Italian restaurant tucked into a dusty, dead-end street in the West Village. A ceiling fan silently circulated stagnant air, and the only noise in the place came from an alcove near the kitchen, where the sous chef was speaking into the pay phone in Spanish, in an aggrieved whisper— embroiled, from what I could decipher, in an argument with his mother.

Between bites of salad, Catherine relayed stories—about knitting, and couture, and academia, and the very strange convergence between them—and thanks to her soft voice and the heat and stillness of the afternoon, listening to her I was lulled into a trancelike state. When, hours later, Catherine showed me samples of the garments she'd been speaking so eloquently about, I was struck to recognize, again, the enormous potential of knitting. Nothing knit by anyone I'd interviewed—Catherine most certainly included—had so far failed to amaze me with its beauty, its originality, its ingenuity.

CATHERINE LOWE

All knitters enjoy knitting, but one who hasn't watched her own colored design growing from her needles hasn't had all the joy of craft.

—ROSE WILDER LANE, WOMAN'S DAY BOOK OF AMERICAN NEEDLEWORK, 1963

My mother and my grandmother were both extraordinary dressmakers—not by profession but by passion. I had, from the time I was born, amazing clothes that were made for me. There's a photograph of me when I was about two years old, wearing this exquisite dress that has been smocked with silk, and I'm in the yard, playing with a hose, covered in mud. My mother also knit, and I would sit next to her, and she would say, "This is a knit stitch; this is a purl stitch; there's only one way to cast on and it's this way, and there's only one way to decrease and it's that way."

Then one day I said, "I want to make a sweater." We went to the local store and I picked out a pattern for a Bavarian sweater with ten colors in it. I knit the sweater—it still fits; I was a very tall kid. And that sort of started it. I guess if there's anything about that first sweater, I didn't like the way the seams looked on it. And I probably did a regular cast-on, so the rib at the bottom is loose. Now I would do an invisible cast-on; I would work the rib a different way so it would have a lot of integrity. I first started doing what I call "couture knitting"—finishing edges, constructing projects in different ways—to cover up what I thought was bad knitting, and I have ended up developing techniques that a lot of people have been happy to learn.

I coined the term "couture knitting" to identify and distinguish what I do. A lot of people knit for the process; I knit for the end product. My audience is probably about 2 percent of the knitters out there. What I do is not leisure. I love it; it relaxes me, but I don't think it relaxes a lot of people. The basic techniques are not basic techniques; they're the basic techniques of my Couture Knitting Workshop. You have to be willing to be precise; you have to be willing to be a lot of things that a lot of knitters aren't. I say to people that they may not like this approach to knitting, but my hope is that there's something in the Workshop they can use. I don't think anyone has ever left saying that it was completely useless—even the most dyed-in-the-wool free-form knitters have found something that appeals to them.

I've developed techniques for constructing and finishing garments that are comparable to those used by fashion houses. Having had the experience with my family of finely made garments, I looked at what distinguishes haute couture and thought through the logic of some of the techniques of pattern drafting and altering in textiles, and translated that into knitting. I think about the way the garment is going to look, about what the construction of the garment is going to be; in other words, I know, with one or two exceptions, how I'm going to finish the garment. If I don't know, I do a prototype, and that tells me what I should do. Then I go back and rework the pattern and put into it all the things I realized from the prototype.

When I was developing my techniques, I decided I wanted to finish every join. Even when you're knitting perpendicular to the garment piece, there is, at the point where you pick up stitches, something I call a "raw join." I developed a way of knitting something that looks like passementerie, almost like a braid. I put that in the ditch where the two garment pieces meet, to fill it.

A lot of designers are interested in surface, and they see surface as either painting or texture. I'm interested in the garment as construction; I'm much more of an architect than a painter. I'm interested in the way a garment fits a body. I do a couple things with fit that are characteristic of my work: shaping, for example, particularly around the armholes and the shoulders. This transforms the way a garment fits without sacrificing ease of wear and comfort. I lower the shoulders by five inches, which means that the garment looks like nothing when it lies flat, but when it's hanging on the body, it establishes a flattering line that looks very strong and fits wonderfully. There's no bulk on the shoulder then, but you have to adjust the sleeve so it isn't enormous. I basically give a dolman shape to the garment, and I've been experimenting with gussets that will allow movement but also force the garment pieces into positions that will make them necessarily slimming on the body. A garment hangs from the shoulders. If it doesn't fit from there, it's not going to look good. A lot of people don't realize that—they think of "fitted" as something that happens down here, at the widest part of the body.

When I do a design and write a pattern, I think about some of the idiosyncrasies I have encountered in my workshops. If I know that a majority of knitters tend to do X or Y, I try to work that into my thinking. I try to make the patterns in such a way that a large number of knitters will be able to execute them fairly proficiently and professionally, and to make sure that any question that might arise in a knitter's mind is already answered by the pattern. In commercial patterns, for example, if there are two fronts, the right front will be described, and for the left front the pattern will say, "Work as for right side, and reverse shaping." In my patterns, every decrease is described and every increase is described, because there are reasons for them—some increases are more flexible than others. When I write a pattern, the directions for the garment process are five to six pages; the directions for the construction and finishing are thirteen to fifteen pages. I'm trying to make a high level of execution available to any knitter who wants it.

The same way that some people will not vary from a recipe—if it calls for a ¼ teaspoon, they're going to make *sure* it's a ¼ teaspoon—that's the way a lot of people knit. So much the better. The pity is that patterns are not written to respond to that. If a pattern says to pick up eighty stitches but it doesn't tell you where or how, the knitter is not necessarily going to be able to produce the kind of garment they want. A lot of people feel overwhelmed when they look at my patterns; there's a lot of information in them. But if someone is up to the technical task, which is not necessarily a very high level, it will probably turn out the way they want it to turn out. If you can knit, and you have the time and can afford beautiful fiber, you can make a garment that's worthy of a designer label.

The number of times I've heard women say they've made a garment but it looked awful! It may simply be a matter of placing a color in the wrong place. I had this lady at a workshop recently who wanted to adapt my techniques to another design. In the picture she showed me, the lightest color was placed exactly on the hip—very few women can wear that and have it look flattering. I took the same detail and ran it up the back, so it wasn't lost. How many times have you looked at the knitting books that come out every season, and the designs have heavy work around the hips, which is precisely where it shouldn't be, or huge cuffs that fall right at the widest part of a woman's body? I'm very sensitive to that, to the way a garment, if it's designed properly, can change a woman's appearance.

My inspiration comes from designers, especially Giorgio Armani, because he is able to flatter a very large number of women with the way he cuts garments. There are small things that he does—he can put a sleeve into an arm unlike anyone. I'm fascinated by the way he's been able to work flat pieces into three dimensions. I've actually introduced some of the elements of his design into my knitting. Someone whose work I think is fabulous, but I'm still trying to figure out what the knitting approximation would be, is Madeleine Vionnet; she does these beautiful draped garments that are often cut on the bias, and fit perfectly, and flatter the body. She's a great inspiration for the way she can transform something very, very simple. I admire Fortuny for his combinations of color, and I would love to find a way to get knitted fabric to drape like his fabrics. He uses handblown glass to hold it down; I could do it with beading, and I thought about that—an allover beaded evening jacket.

I sell my designs in kits, along with all the things needed to complete them. I try to make sure that everything I use to make my patterns I can provide. If there are buttons on the garment, there are backing buttons in the kit; you don't want the buttons to go through yarn; you want them to go through the spaces between stitches, and you need to attach a button to something on the underside. Hooks and eyes are in the kits. I used to go so far as to put in a needle threaded with either cotton or silk, because the buttons shouldn't be sewn on with yarn. I try to limit the availability of my kits; I think it's important to discontinue them after a certain amount of time so that dozens of knitters aren't knitting the same colorway, because I want knitters to feel that they can create something unique.

I taught at Williams and other colleges for many years, but I was completely disillusioned with academics—the politics of the profession and universities. I left academics and took a year off to decide what to do. I wrote a two-hundred-page novel and decided, "Hmmm, there's something going on here." In the meantime, I had moved to Washington, D.C., because my parents were ill and I wanted to be with them. I started hanging around the yarn shop, and they offered me a job. I became their in-house designer, and I started teaching, and soon I was doing something I never imagined.

Outside Florence is an institution called the Fondazione Lisio, and it's basically a weaving institute. They make some of the finest fabrics in the world for clothing and interior decoration; the walls are covered with photographs of European monarchies and aristocracies, wearing gowns made out of their brocades and cut-silk velvets. The education department of the Fondazione Lisio is located right next to one of the mills. I had a friend who was the director and also a great knitter, and she asked me to develop a knitting program to complement their weaving program. We tried it for a year. We announced the curriculum and nobody was interested, because in Europe, you don't go to school to learn to knit—your grandmother teaches you how to knit.

At any rate, it may have been the fact that knitting was more accepted in Italy or it may have been because I was out of the pressure of an academic environment that I was finally able to come out of the closet with my knitting for the first time. I would never have knit when I was involved in academia—never, *never!* They would have thought that I wasn't a serious scholar.

I still think of myself as a scholar in many ways, and my life as an intellectual life, and that isn't going to change. Mine is a very scholarly approach to knitting, and I don't quite know how else to frame it. I try to be as absolutely thorough as possible. I've started publishing a knitting journal, *The Ravell'd Sleeve.* The purpose of the journal is to take the very first elements of couture knitting all the way through so that someone who is reading the journals regularly can incorporate the techniques into their knitting. After the first issue, they're ready for the second issue—for the next step. It builds on itself. In each issue, there is a technical article and a small project pattern—it's called a practicum—that I develop to put into practice what I've talked about in the technical piece. It's a puzzle: How am I going to devise a pattern that makes use of the information in the technical piece but doesn't make use of anything I haven't talked about yet?

Here's one of my pieces, a vest in Rose Stitch Fabric. You can wear it with a brooch to close it; you can wear it without the brooch, so it hangs; or you can wear it upside down. That way, it becomes a shrug with a shawl collar. It's fun, because you can wear it rightside up during the day, then decide you're going to dinner and turn it around. I always work from paper—I fold paper like origami, and that's how I worked this out. I had a basic idea of how I wanted this garment to work, so I started folding to see what I had to do, where I had to add, where things had to be, because I can write on the paper and I can see what the range of motion is going to be.

I would like to get to a place where my designs are a wardrobe option that can stand beside couture jackets—notice that I don't call my pieces sweaters; that's inimical to my design and approach. It's a lofty aim, and I don't pretend to have achieved it. It makes people laugh, but I always say that I don't want the garment to wear me; I want to wear the garment. It should enhance the wearer, not show off skill. I don't want a person to look at me and ask, "Did you make that?" I want them to say, "What a lovely jacket."

Rumors

If you wish to see it before your own eyes
Have no fixed thoughts either for or against it.
—Seng-Tsan,
"On Believing in Mind"

All spring, there were rumors circulating in New York about the fates of knitters in airports and on airplanes—every one of them grim. I went into an eyeglass store to have a pair of sunglasses repaired for my trip to California, and the guy working in the place told me a story about a flight he'd made to Canada a few weeks earlier: "There was this old woman waiting on line to go through the security check. An *old* lady, about seventy-five. She gets up to the security check, and they start going through her bags. They find a whole shopping bag full of knitting, and balls of yarn, and some knitting needles. The needles are still attached to the sweater she's making. She's obviously a knitter, you know? The security guy says to the old lady, 'You're going to have to come with me.' Gruff, kind of mean. Without any explanation at all, he takes her by the arm, takes her bag of knitting, and walks her into a back room. And the old lady is crying, 'What did I do?'"

I certainly had no intention of giving up knitting for the two weeks of my trip, but after hearing this story and others, I had to concede that trying to knit on the five-hour flight to Los Angeles, or even trying to squirrel a pair of needles into my carry-on suitcase, was probably a bad idea. I decided I would pack only yarn and a small stack of Xeroxes from the Barbara Walker pattern book and buy needles when I arrived in L.A.

It took me a couple days, though, to make my way to my first L.A. yarn shop—Suss Designs on Beverly Boulevard, known for its celebrity

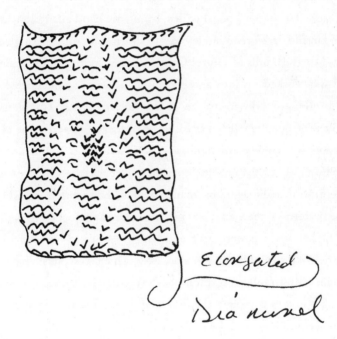

Elongated
Diamond

clientele and high-end dresses and sweaters and baby clothes—which was recommended to me by Nancy Lenehan on the morning we met at the Farmers Market. Dawdling around the shop, I fawned over a pair of tiny red knitted Mary Janes and chatted for a few minutes with one of the shop's teachers. Finally: needles. Almost everyone I'd spoken to had raved about circulars, and I'd been eager to try them. I selected an 8", size #8 bamboo needle from an enormous rack, let the shop girl ring me up, and then practically jogged out of there, eager to get someplace where I could give it a trial spin.

An hour later, I was sitting on the porch of a friend's house, under the shade of a riotous bougainvillea, trying my hand at an Elongated Diamond in the dark green Jamie Harmon yarn. The surrounding environment—the lush hills of Laurel Canyon—was decidedly a soothing one, but I was worked up into an aggravated lather. The circulars couldn't have been more awkward to use, at least for swatching. The plastic cord between the needles twisted as I knit, then snapped back in the opposite direction at inconvenient moments, often causing a couple stitches to pop off one tip of the needle. Stopping to replace the stitches, I lost my concentration and forgot how many stitches I had knitted and which line in the pattern I'd reached. I was getting better at recognizing the look of my stitches—which were knit and which were purl—so it hadn't yet been necessary to pull out and start over, which was a nice change from previous pattern-following attempts. Nevertheless, it took me two teeth-gritting hours to complete the diamond. Instead of feeling any pride in the final result, however, I was decidedly ambivalent about it. The green rectangle enveloping only a very vague diamond of the same coloring looked bland and uninteresting. Not even the feel of the luxurious, supple angora blend, brought to my cheek for caresses, could raise my enthusiasm above a shrug.

Maru Mori brought me
a pair
of socks
that she knit with her
shepherd's hands.
Two socks as soft
as rabbit fur.
I thrust my feet
inside them
as if they were
two
little boxes
knit
from threads
of sunset
and sheepskin.

My feet were
two woolen
fish
in those outrageous socks,
two gangly,
navy-blue sharks

impaled
on a golden thread,
two giant blackbirds,
two cannons:
thus
were my feet
honored
by
those
heavenly
socks.
They were
so beautiful
I found my feet
unlovable
for the very first time,
like two crusty old
firemen, firemen
unworthy
of that embroidered
fire,
those incandescent
socks.

—PABLO NERUDA, FROM "ODE TO A PAIR OF SOCKS"

("ODA A LOS CALCETINES," TRANSLATED BY KEN KRABBENHOFT.)

6.

A Spring Day:
San Francisco

I learned about Artfibers, a yarn shop and knitter's hangout in San Francisco, when I was planning my trip to California. I'd already rounded up plenty of people to interview, but on a whim, I sent out an e-mail mentioning my book and my trip. Perhaps it would be possible to drop in for a visit? I asked.

I would eventually, and more than once, have cause to celebrate my decision to contact the shop. Its first delightful outcome was a letter— spontaneous, unsolicited—from Nyle Seabright, who, with his wife, Roxanne, owns Artfibers. Though I would never actually meet Nyle, I felt an almost immediate affinity for him, so thoughtful and heartfelt was his letter. I read it over and over and hoped it was a harbinger of more inspired stories to come from the fog-driven city on the bay.

NYLE SEABRIGHT

Make the Universe your companion, always bearing in mind the true nature of things—mountains and rivers, trees and grasses, and humanity—and enjoy the falling blossoms and scattering leaves.

—Bashō on Poetry,

"Learn from the Pine"

I came to California in 1968 with two other expatriate philosophy students from Minnesota, all of us in search of spirituality. They joined Zen Center and became senior monks; I never got the drift of it. About that time, Zen Center's founder, Shunryu Suzuki, published a book called *Zen Mind, Beginner's Mind.* In some ways, the therapeutic value of knitting is greatest when it can be approached as a beginner. I think of the core concept of Islam, which translates literally to "surrender," in the sense of giving oneself up to something greater. The adventure of beginning is that it breaks the mold of life, allowing a rigid sense of self to be set aside so that the spirit can open into a new form (like a caterpillar becoming a butterfly).

The most important part of this kind of inner journey is that it does not become rigid. My friends left Zen Center to follow Chogyam Trungpa, and his book *Cutting Through Spiritual Materialism* says a great deal about not taking accomplishment too seriously. My hope is that people will be open to a spiritual dimension of knitting, but also that they will not measure their progress along this path and somehow feel deficient.

At Artfibers, we have cultivated an environment of encouragement. That pretty much sums up our objective on a spiritual level. There are sample balls of every yarn, and anyone can come in at any time and play with them at no charge. They get to keep what they make at the swatching table. For them, nothing remains as an impediment, not even money. The adventure can move forward, loop by loop. I think this is the state that Suzuki Roshi was referring to when he said, "We must always treasure our beginner's mind." The great thing about knitting is that, with nothing more than two sticks and a string, you can always find a new adventure, no matter how accomplished you are.

Six weeks ago, my mother died. She was a lifelong knitter of great skill, and in many ways it was her influence that led us to start Artfibers. I remember so clearly on the day before she died—a really difficult and exhausting day for all of us—that at the first opportunity she asked for her knitting. She was making chemo caps for the American Cancer Society and anyone else along the way who would accept one, and had a long list of people to give hats to. Looking back on her life, I can see that knitting was a vehicle for generosity. She was a child of abject Depression poverty, but she always felt that it was possible to find a way to give something to someone. Not only possible but necessary, and not for any doctrinaire reason. She would often knit with yarn that someone didn't want, and it wasn't great stuff. But the gesture of producing something meaningful out of something valueless was part of the attraction for her.

Mom had a difficult life and probably did find great solace and healing in knitting. But she would have found it strange to see that as a goal. She had very little interest in her own status in life. The motivation was always the vision of a smile when someone received an occasionless gift, especially from a stranger, even better if they would never meet. Knitting made that possible for her. Generosity has its own healing force, especially when the circle reaches out in mysterious and surprising ways. We begin to heal society—only kindness has the power to overcome anger.

My first memory is of holding a skein of yarn, and fiber has been a recurring part of my life, even when it was in the form of Kevlar and carbon when I was making high-performance sporting goods. In the late '70s, I heard Buckminster Fuller talking about fiber and structure at a seminar at the Sheraton Palace Hotel in San Francisco, about a block from where our store eventually located. At one point, he asked someone from the audience to come to the stage and tie a simple knot in a piece of rope that he held. Then he loosened the knot and slid one end of the rope further through, moving the knot closer to the other end. He asked the person if it was the same knot, and of course they said it was, since it consisted of the same loops.

Bucky then challenged that view by pointing out how the molecules in the human body are constantly being replaced, yet we still think of people as being the same people. The sameness is of pattern, and he used this example to introduce the concept of "patterned integrity," which he felt was the basic building block of the universe. I am reminded of trees when I knit—they are made up of carbon-based molecules, and the carbon is drawn from carbon dioxide in the atmosphere and precipitated by light via photosynthesis. Knitting is structure that appears out of thin air, like a tree or a galaxy precipitating from interstellar vacuum. These thoughts lead me to feel at one with the mystery of creation when knitting—perhaps as much spirituality as I will ever have in me, but enough.

 Roxanne wrote to me shortly thereafter, all enthusiasm. She'd be delighted if I'd visit, she said, and as incentive, she rounded up some of her very best customers and teachers: Joan Merle, an artist and designer who wears glasses that lend her an owlish expression and one of her own knit hats set debonairly atop her head; Katherine Bacher-Fares—also an artist—a native of Switzerland and a new mother (she was glad for a reason to leave the house for a few hours and to engage in "adult" conversation); and Amy Backos and Melanie Loew, two young women who teach at and knit for the shop, among other pursuits. Roxanne arranged a morning for us all to meet in the shop before it opened at 10 A.M. (When I did visit—on a sunny day in June that held, still, a bit of spring coolness—I found the flier she'd posted to solicit interviewees, a cheerful yellow card announcing: "Special event at Artfibers!" No one has ever referred to me as a "special event" before or since.)

"This shop is the result of wanting to be in a creative business," Roxanne told me. "Nyle and I decided to be really, really different with our yarn shop by designing our own yarns and having them made for us. We swatch hundreds of samples a year to select maybe thirty lines that we'll have at any one time. It has to be special. We do a lot of testing—swatching, dying, washing, everything—for the yarn's feel, and how interesting it can be, and how interesting it is going to be to dye, and what can we do with it. We're kind of buried in this world. It takes everything we can put into it to make the business go.

"I remember getting a few years into this business and remembering that the same best friend who taught me to knit and I had planned, since seventh grade, to someday start a business together. Her name was French and it meant flower, and my last name then was German, and it meant wool, and we were going to call it Flowers on the Wool, because it was the sixties." Roxanne, at least, if not her old friend Fleur, has managed to realize that long-ago plan. In 2002, Artfibers turned seven years old, and its reputation has spread to many distant cities.

Artfibers

The true joy of knitting is only obtained when it becomes a creative craft.
—MARJORY TILLOTSON,
THE COMPLETE KNITTING BOOK, 1933

ROXANNE SEABRIGHT: All of us here have art backgrounds, and artists can be very secretive about what they do, what their techniques are. Knitting is not competitive; in knitting, everybody's going, "Wow, look what I've found!"

JOAN MERLE: When I learn something new in knitting, I like to share it. Most people who knit do it because they love it; they don't knit to sell their projects. The only time I ever felt that I very much didn't want someone to know how I did something was when I was selling my things in a store. I was very careful to use all different kinds of yarn so no one could figure out what I did. At this point, I don't feel that way, because I'm not trying to be commercial. I'm still learning.

ROXANNE: Maybe that's it, the humbling thing; you never know it all. There's always somebody out there who can wow you with what they do. Why not be generous?

KATHERINE BACHER-FARES: I knit as an artist, maybe for a gallery or to show people what I can do. But once I worked for a designer; she was protective, not toward employees but to outside stores, because there were people who wanted to copy and would have things made in China. As soon as it comes to a business, then it's getting competitive.

JOAN: When you're knitting, you're not creating an assembly line–made thing. What you knit is not going to be exactly like someone else's. You have a different gauge, which is your fingerprint.

ROXANNE: Even if you're working from a pattern, nine times out of ten you'll start it and then say, "Hmmm, I think I'll change this." I think that's true for most knitters.

JOAN: I ran into a design problem on something, and I made it into some other thing. You use your mistakes—it's like somebody gave you a gift. My background is in clothing construction and painting. Knitting encompasses both of those. It's a very tactile way of expressing myself, and I never get tired of it because there's always something new to try. The variety is very inspiring—it's endless.

ROXANNE: Mine is painting and sculpture, and for me, color and texture are everything, so this is really satisfying. I thought when Nyle and I got into this, and I was not getting time to do my other art, that I was going to suffer. I haven't at all.

KATHERINE: I didn't do any other art before knitting, but in Switzerland I never considered myself an artist. There they didn't think that knitting could be an art form. I was just teaching arts and crafts, and knitting was included. I came here and went to a textile arts school, and it just opened up a whole new world. Life in Switzerland was much more rigid compared to here. Here I was compelled to wear a pink sock and a green sock at the same time because I was allowed to do it; nobody would really look—until I met my husband, and then he said, "No, oh, no, no, no. . . ." [laughter]

AMY BACKOS: I studied psychology and studio art, and I went into art therapy. Mostly I did painting, then I learned to knit about five years ago. I worked with kids in Cleveland, and I would try to make up things for them to do, like painting with string.

ROXANNE: I learned to knit in junior high school. My best friend was the oldest of thirteen children, and she knew how to do everything because she had to. She taught me cooking, knitting, crocheting. At that point I was living in a suburb of L.A. and the yarns were horrible—cheap—and they came in bad colors. After spending a lot of hours making things I wanted to throw away because they were so ugly, I just dropped it for a while. Then, when Nyle and I were living in France, we stumbled on some mills that were producing amazing yarns for fashion houses like Chanel. That's what inspired me to get back into knitting—that was what I knew how to do with yarn. Yarn is the reason I'm in this business; my husband and I are the worst yarn junkies you ever saw. My husband is so funny because I'll say, "You know, the store's looking pretty full." "But look," he'll say, "we can get this!" And I then I'm convinced we have to have it.

A woman called the day before yesterday and said, "I started this baby blanket and I'm out of yarn." And I said, "Bring it in, and we'll see what we can do." I couldn't believe it when I saw it. The woman had cast on the right number of stitches, but she was using a lace pattern and she didn't realize what she was supposed to be doing; she kept increasing and increasing and increasing, and she had this beautiful thing that was a big ruffle—she hadn't even realized it. She had used a lot of yarn and done a lot of work. I said, "This is beautiful, but it's not a baby blanket." She decided to rip it out.

AMY: Too bad!

JOAN: I once was making a baby hat for my granddaughter and I did something wrong, and it ended up becoming this big thing. I appliquéd over it and used it as a pillow.

KATHERINE: Part of my knitting is getting away from making everything neat and straight and following patterns. I sometimes use big needles where someone would say, "That's a mistake; you need to use small needles." I basically came away from doing all this in a precise way, and just always work out of my head.

JOAN: When I was studying to be an abstract painter, I was a very symmetrical, follow-the-dots type of person. When I started knitting, I decided I was absolutely *not* going to follow patterns. Now I follow patterns and it's fun, but it's hard to let go of the regimen and what you've learned.

AMY: I started out much more free-form, and now I'm creating designs ahead of time, creating things I can really wear. When I use patterns, it's to learn something new and improve my skill. But when I knit free-form, a much more expressive part of me comes out—the art therapy part of me.

JOAN: I don't allow myself to start knitting until 12 P.M.; I get *The New York Times* every day, and I say, "You're *not* going to start knitting until you've gotten through it."

AMY: I have to put myself on probation also. I can't start any more projects until I've finished the four I've got going.

ROXANNE: I've got it easy, because I get to do all the swatching and testing for the store, so I get my rush from doing that. I always have a real project going, but generally not more than two at the most, because then I'd never finish them.

JOAN: I do more than one project at a time, but I may be making more than one of the same thing in different yarns with different approaches, because I want to use the first piece as a pattern for the second piece. I'm exploring this concept. I just finished a kimono, and I'm thinking of doing the same thing in the same yarn but using a different stitch and playing around with that just to see what will happen.

KATHERINE: I pretty much stick to one project, because they can be huge. I did those wall hangings, *The Four Elements*. I started with the Water, then Fire, then Air, then I made the Earth. [The women laugh.] They were really a long-term project. The Earth took me forever; I was really glad when I finished it. [The women laugh again.] I knitted them on the machine, so that's different. I knitted long swatches and put them together in one long piece. I used paper, plastic bags, wire, fabrics, beads, buttons, leaves, shells, pop-tops from cans. When I moved to California, I was overwhelmed by all the disposable stuff: containers, cups, pop-tops. It's not good for the environment, but I can use it in my art.

I don't know how big a piece is going to be at the beginning. But with the Earth, I realized there is a point at which I have to make the decision: Now it's finished. Because I could have gotten carried away. I have to finish it no matter what.

JOAN: The thing about knitting that's different from anything else is that you have to develop your own dimension. Your gauge is different, and you can wind up with all different sizes. Whereas with painting, you stretch your canvas and there it is. You have control over so much more when you knit.

[Melanie Loew rushes into the room, looking slightly sheepish about arriving late. She's wearing a blue cotton hat of her own invention—a sort of rounded fishing-style hat with a belt and buckle around the crown, above the brim.]

JOAN: Just *making* is a wonderful thing to do.

KATHERINE: It's a passion.

AMY: For me, a big part of it is keeping myself company.

JOAN: Right now I'm working on something, and I can't even have people around.

AMY: But I still consider you part of my knitting community. . . .

JOAN: I think that's because we can discuss knitting. But as far as the actual process is concerned, I can't go to a café to knit with lots of people around. I did that once, and I really hated it. At that point, I was knitting completely creatively, and people were talking about their personal problems and knitting, and I thought, *That's not why I'm here.* That kind of sitting around with the girls really turns me off.

MELANIE: Amy and I get together on Saturdays.

AMY: Every Saturday we watch *Sex and the City* together and knit. We stock up on water in case of emergencies!

MELANIE: We knit, and sometimes we analyze the TV, and sometimes we do therapy. I think that the way we approach knitting is the way we approach life. How you do anything is how you do everything.

AMY: There's knitting for all personalities: There are people who rip everything out, people who are relaxed; you can be tidy. . . .

ROXANNE: You can take it any direction you want. There's a phrase my husband was telling me about from one of the Zen masters: "We must always treasure our beginner's mind." I think that's part of what we love about knitting; we are able to always begin something new—new technique, new yarns, new experience every time. You never will learn it all. Knitting is a microcosm. We can see everything there is to life just by studying this medium. I think part of the reason people have been attracted to knitting—and I swear, every generation says this—is that life is getting crazier. It's harder and harder to find a way to fit the kind of creativity we all need into our lives.

 Terri Wong, a longstanding Artfibers regular, called me before my trip to San Francisco to tell me that she wouldn't be able to make it to the morning breakfast meeting at the shop—it was too early, and she had to go to work. We agreed to meet a couple days later.

I arrived a few minutes before our scheduled rendezvous to find that the shop, even during prime business hours, was an oasis of serenity. Outside, downtown San Francisco teemed with men and women in suits rushing for buses and to cross streets before lights turned red. Inside Art-fibers, music twinkled from speakers as Amy worked a sweater pattern on the computer; several women mutely browsed the yarn shelves; another woman sat trancelike at a table near the enormous front windows, a Tupperware container filled with sample yarns open before her, knitting a tiny swatch on tiny needles with a pale pink, fine-gauge spun silk-and-mohair blend. Terri bustled in from beyond, wearing one of the dance-inspired, fitted knit tops for which she's celebrated in these here parts. The atmosphere at Artfibers rustled for a moment before it seemed to adjust ever-so-subtly to her presence (or she eased into its slower respirings), and calm, and a pervasive hush—softening even our conversation—returned.

Terri Wong

My family is from mainland China. Needlework in China was a way for women to make money outside the house right until the Communists took over, and then of course all that changed. It was pretty traditional for my grandmother's generation, something she learned in school. My grandmother wanted to get me into sewing, and since I was such a big failure at that, she paid for my knitting lessons when I was ten years old. I learned from a teacher down in Santa Cruz—I thought it was fun. I'm an only child and didn't have any siblings or cousins to play with, so it was a nice change from reading. If I wasn't hanging out at the library, I was knitting.

I come from an abusive family, and I spent my summers and my school holidays with my grandmother. Knitting was a way to ground myself. I'd make things for dolls, but I never made anything for myself, mostly because I didn't really have access to good-quality wool; my mother always dragged me to places like Woolworth's. I didn't start making anything that remotely resembled a garment until I took off fifty pounds. One hundred and fifty pounds and five feet tall—I was a little round.

My grandmother died at the age of 101. I remember the last thing she took with her into the nursing home was an afghan I had made. It was so old, and it was falling apart. My aunts kept trying to take it away from her, and she kept saying, "No, I'm taking it with me." So she took it with her and it stayed folded at the foot of her bed. She couldn't use it, and she refused to let me take it away long enough to let me mend it or add to it. One of the last things I made for her was a sweater jacket. My grandmother was six inches taller than me, and after she died I took it back and sized it down so that it would fit me. We had a special relationship. She really appreciated the arts. When everybody else gave me a hard time about being an opera singer, she was the only one who supported me. Of course, the first time she heard it . . . She thought it was going to be Chinese opera, which sounds like cats yelling. But she liked the music, and once you explained the plot to her, it kind of grew on her. I'll probably go back to it after my daughter is in college.

I'm currently working as a paralegal. It doesn't make much sense to work nights and weekends when your kid is in school—I would never see her. It's a nice break to be able to come in to Artfibers and teach on my lunch hour, to have that sort of change of mind. Everyone in my office knows what I do. They say, "Oh, you're going to go eat, huh?" I've been knitting all along anyway. When I was doing opera, I was in one production during which five or six of us were doing something else backstage: someone was quilting, someone was making a sweater, someone was weaving. There's a lot of downtime during the rehearsals because you aren't always on stage, and even if you are, you aren't always singing. "Stand here for half an hour!"

A lot of people come in here at lunchtime just to knit and talk. I think that's what women used to do anyway, the whole quilting-bee idea of sitting around and exchanging anecdotes, catching up on your families. There's nothing wrong with that—it's something I enjoy. Before I started teaching here four years ago, the only other person I taught to knit was my daughter, Miyako. She was nine or ten at the time. When she was ready to learn, she wanted me to get her a book, and she taught herself how to knit continental-style. I always tell people, "She's right-handed but she knits left-handed." She just found that it made more sense to her. I don't care; it all comes out looking the same—there's more than one way to get through the same project.

A couple years ago, I made a sweater for my boyfriend, and Miyako helped. We have about the same gauge, although I think she had to use a different size needle. It was fun to do. She started out making clothes for Beanie Babies in middle school and sold them for extra present money at Christmas. I suggested that maybe she'd like to help me make this sweater for Tom and she said, "Oh, yeah!" And I said, "It's a lot of yardage, honey; he's six-two and two hundred pounds; he's not a little guy. *A big sweater.*" But it was straight knitting, not anything fancy or with cables—straight stockinette stitch, so it was no problem. We combined two different shades, so it came out kind of tweedy.

When I was seventeen, I became interested in Buddhism—a quirky form of Japanese Buddhism founded by Nichiren Daishonen. The combination of Buddhism and knitting helped to center me in terms of what

I wanted to do with my life and figuring out how to stop abusing myself. It was enough that my family was doing it; I didn't need to do it to myself, too. Nichiren Daishonin was kind of a rebel—he managed to get himself exiled by the government for preaching such radical things as women can achieve enlightenment. I found that kind of attractive, being the black sheep in my family. I like to quote from one of his letters: "More valuable than the treasures in the storehouse are the treasures of the body, and the treasures of the heart are most valuable of all." My daughter keeps asking me, "What do you mean by 'treasures of the storehouse'?" Position, title, and "body" are elements of good health and being attractive. "Treasures of the heart" are things that you can't see with your eyes, the things that are more important. My daughter and I tend to make all our gifts, which is also a way of giving something of your own heart. When you make something for someone, you've taken the time to know a person, to know what they like—their colors, what they like to wear, what their lifestyle is like, little things like that. There's more thought in it than if you buy something in a store because it's expensive.

The things I make for myself are a little different, but it's also fun to make things that are custom-designed for your body. We all have different body types—I'm really short-waisted, but I have long legs. Some of my pieces are dance-related, like this little wrap top. It's just fun experimenting, taking a different kind of material and seeing what happens with it. Sometimes I say, "I want to work with this color" or "I want something to wear with this." My daughter saw some variegated yarn and immediately decided she had to have a tank top. So, she's going to have a tank top with twisted ribbing. I seldom pick a pattern that's very complicated anymore. After a while, since I know my body shape and my daughter's, you get to know what will work—there's not much point in trying anything else, because it won't look good on us. I knit mostly tops; occasionally I'll do a jacket. I stay away from skirts and pants. Buying store-bought pants is less difficult for me than buying a top. If worse comes to worst, I can always wear black pants.

Knitting, like practicing Buddhism, is addictive because it's meditative. I don't knit at the same time that I pray, but the combination of doing both activities really helps keep me grounded. You can link it to the memory of a family member you miss—I do think of my grandmother when I knit—or the whole idea that we really are all interconnected: It doesn't matter what race we are, what religion we practice, because we're human beings; we do all have that in common. And that basic respect should always be there.

 I found both Baruch Gould, Director of Public Programs at the C. G. Jung Institute, and Eddie Kaufman, Director of Prevention for the Youth Leadership Institute (and a biker—the proud owner of a black 2000 Shadow American Touring Classic), through the ever-helpful Roxanne at Artfibers; they are most faithful regulars. "Lots of men knit," I'd heard over and over, from women (always women) in knitting shops everywhere I'd gone, despite much evidence (or lack thereof) to the contrary. Here, at least—at last—are two of them.

BARUCH GOULD

*[S]o looneywise our hero, or villain,
or madcap fool, call him what you
will, wandered through fields
and woodlands thinking out
all the wonderful things he would
make one day when he had mastered
the knitters craft.*

—JAMES NORBURY, *KNITTING IS*

AN ADVENTURE, 1958

I study astrology. I believe astrology is one valid way of getting a handle on the "energies" in one's life. The planet Venus represents attraction: what attracts us and what we are attracted to. Appreciation of beauty falls under Venus's energy. My Venus is in the fifth house (the house of creativity and self-expression) in the sign of Capricorn. Capricorn is the fixed Earth sign, and it wants to ground energy. My love of knitting and what I like to knit is typical of a Venus in Capricorn: I love three-dimensional art; I love art that is useful. I love glass vases; I love pottery; I love color that can be worn as clothing or decoration. To me, knitting is taking color and turning it into something one can drape over the body.

I learned to knit here in San Francisco about six years ago; I was taught by another man, and I took to it with a passion. I never thought about knitting before that time, but I was intrigued. I had some trouble at first, especially with purling—I often forgot to put the yarn in back when I purled, so I knit with lots of yarn-overs (holes).

When I walked into Artfibers for the first time, I literally danced around the store. It was *my* kind of place. It vibrated with life and creativity. Roxanne and Nyle, each in their separate ways, have great creative energy, which I found invigorating and supporting. Their encouragement was essential to me as I experimented with combining different yarns and making up my own designs.

Knitting has become an art form for me; it is like painting. I have come to see my knitting as wearable art, not just pieces of clothing. I love the Fauvist art represented by Matisse. Instead of putting bold colors on canvas with oil paint, I put bold colors on the body using yarn. I also love natural fibers, fibers that are connected to living things—trees, animals, plants—and the combination of color and fiber, and deciding how to combine the two from the inspiration of the unconscious. This is the joy of knitting for me.

Sometimes I get an idea to knit something by having a color—or colors—surface up to my consciousness. I think to myself, *I want to make something yellow; I want to create a yellow* whatever. Often I start knitting, and it takes on a life of its own. I think I am going to do one thing, but my fingers do something else. I believe my knitting comes from my creative unconscious; that's why I love to do free-form.

When I teach classes in free-form knitting at Artfibers, the typical reaction from the class is one of joyous freedom: "You mean I don't have to follow a pattern? You mean I can make it up as I go along?" Most people feel liberated. Some don't. They can't imagine *not* having the blueprint; they find comfort in the literalness of patterns. I knit with patterns, too. Right now I am working on a complicated multi-cable sweater with merino wool and tussah silk. Each row *must* be exactly precise. The sweater will be gorgeous. But I am also working on hats, berets, and scarves that get all sorts of colors thrown into them, and no two look alike.

I was sitting in an airport waiting area a few years ago, knitting. I saw a woman watching me from across the room. She finally got up and came over to me and said, "I never saw a man knit before." I said, "We can do this, too, you know." She laughed and expressed her amazement that I was a male and obviously a good knitter. I think knitting does come from the feminine side. It is not an accident that many ancient cultures associated spinning and knitting with the Great Mother, especially in her form as Fate. Spinning and knitting are transformational acts, like fire transforms matter from one kind of thing to another, so knitting transforms raw material into beauty. Knitting is an alchemical process. I think for men to knit is for them to be in direct contact with that feminine side of themselves. Men have a feminine side—most often undeveloped, especially in our culture. But I expect to see more men knitting in years to come. This will be a *very* good and healing thing for men to do.

EDDIE KAUFMAN

*Only a man would knit a hammock
with shovel handles for needles and
manila rope for yarn.*

—BACK JACKET OF *THE MANLY ART OF
KNITTING* BY DAVE FOUGNER, 1972

When I was working on the Marin AIDS Project, the textile craft supply shop, Dharma Trading, was about a block away from my office. I would walk by the store several times a week and see a sign that said FREE LEARN-TO-KNIT CLASSES. I didn't think much of it for a year or so. There were a couple things that happened to make me change my mind. First, I realized that I had a lot of anxiety; I really wanted to change something in my life to help lower my stress level, which I think was a result of dealing with issues that come with working with clients who are HIV-positive. The other thing was that at work, I was obliged to attend a number of meetings. During these meetings, I would become very fidgety and very bored. I wanted something I could do with my hands. Then one day, when I was walking by Dharma Trading, it clicked: Knitting was something I could do to address both issues. I resolved to attend a knitting class during my next lunch hour.

I was expecting more of a class format, but in fact, the "class" was just a table to which people brought their knitting projects. I was a little nervous; I was the only man at the table, and the only person under fifty. But everyone was great and very supportive. The instructor showed me how to cast on and then how to knit continental-style. Then I sat around the table and chatted and tried knitting. I really enjoyed my time at the store. I would go there on as many of my lunch breaks as I could. The women I met at the table were friendly; we would talk a lot about our lives and the projects we were working on.

I fell in love with knitting right off. I took to it amazingly well and got rather fast in a short period of time. I was never very coordinated growing up, so when I started getting the hang of it, I was a little surprised. I also began to realize that this was an avenue that I could follow to express my creativity. I had found my medium.

All of a sudden, my life changed. I no longer dreaded meetings but looked forward to them, because I would bring my knitting in and work on whatever project I had going at the time. I also found that knitting helped me to stay focused; my mind wouldn't wander, and I concentrated more on the topics we discussed. I found that I was really enjoying myself.

My first project was a scarf—I figured it would be simple—which I started on a trip to Hawaii. I quickly discovered how much I enjoyed knitting at the airport. We had a couple of delays but I wasn't particularly bothered, because I had my knitting. The long flight was the perfect place to continue my project. I was stuck sitting for several hours with nothing to do but knit. I actually finished the scarf by the time I'd gotten back from my trip. I gave it to a supervisor of mine to thank her for her work with me.

Since then, I've always brought my knitting on planes. As a result, flight attendants, particularly the women, always give me a lot of attention. We end up having conversations that start off about the knitting but quickly become about their lives. I think I get better service because of it. Once, though, after September 11, I had the captain come up to me and inform me that she would have to take away my knitting. She was really embarrassed, because it was clear that I wasn't a threat, but somebody had complained that they were afraid I would use my wooden knitting needles as weapons. I must have looked very threatening knitting a sweater!

After that first scarf, I decided I wanted to make a sweater for my partner. This was in August, and I thought that if I started it then, I could have it done in time to give it to him for Christmas. I found wool I really liked and got to work. Little did I realize how much I would enjoy it and how fast it would go. Instead of taking four or five months, I had the sweater completed in four weeks. I ended up giving it to him for his birthday instead of Christmas. Since then, I have knitted numerous sweaters, and I always try to find patterns that will teach me something new.

One of my most exciting and challenging pieces was a *chuppa* (a Jewish wedding canopy) that I made for some friends. I wanted to give them something personal that came from my heart and my hands. They were really flattered. When I asked them what they wanted with the *chuppa*, they told me that they wanted a relatively neutral color in a beige or white, so as not to take away from the wedding and the surroundings, but they did agree to a splash of color around the border. In making the swatches, I tried to have an array of yarns for them to choose from, including metallic fibers, cottons, wools, linens, and other light-colored

yarns. As a result, I had about nine different swatches with three different gauge sizes: from #7, #9, and #11 needles. Given that this was going
to be my largest project, I was hoping that my friends would choose the
#11s. They choose the #9s, though, and really liked the look of the linen
yarn. So with these directives in mind, I began work on the tapestry.

While working on the body of the *chuppa,* I found the perfect yarn
for the border. Artfibers has a number of unique and original yarns. One

Persian Lace

day, I found a yarn that was beautiful and multicolored, that was created
out of the remnants of silk saris made in Nepal. When the hand loomers
make the saris, there are always small fragments that get cut or that fall
to the ground. The weavers had spun these pieces into yarn, which was
exquisite. Each skein was unique and variegated. I thought this would be
the perfect complement of color to the neutral *chuppa.*

I then created a pattern that would give the piece strength, because it had to be held up on poles and needed to be 4' x 6', and also let light shine through, because the wedding was to be held outside. I also wanted to try out some new stitches. And because of the enormity of the piece and the relatively short time in which to create it, I wanted stitches that would create some length in the piece. Keeping this all in mind, I decided to create a repeating pattern using three basic stitches. I used a simple stockinette stitch for six inches; then, for another six inches, I switched to a stitch that requires you to wrap the yarn around the needle after the stitch, which creates space between the rows; and finally, I used a simple lace stitch for six rows. I alternated these stitches throughout the whole piece. For the border, I decided to create a one-inch piece and sew it to the *chuppa*.

The project took me four months, and I worked on it nonstop. I was worried, because this was going to be the largest piece I ever knitted, and I had a definite deadline. The wedding took place in late summer, in August 2001, which is a beautiful time in the San Francisco Bay Area. Summers can be very cold and overcast, but toward the end of the summer, the weather turns comfortable and clear. The wedding took place outside in Tilden Park in Oakland, with trees and a creek in the background. I finished the *chuppa* with a couple weeks to spare. It was a nice touch, because friends created many other parts of the wedding ceremony—six of us were asked to give our interpretation of a blessing; another friend, a silversmith, made silver wine goblets; another friend did the flowers—so the *chuppa* fit in beautifully.

Lately, I have really enjoyed looking at knitted pieces, figuring out how they were made, then replicating them. I have been working on a triangular hair wrap—sort of a kerchief—for a friend. She had one she really loved, but it was starting to fray. I got the opportunity to reverse-engineer it. I realized her original piece of orange wool was probably machine-made, but I figured out the pattern and the stitch—that was the hardest part. I went to Artfibers, and they helped me look through the stitch book to determine what it was. I found out it was honeycomb, which was exciting and relatively easy. From that point, it was easy to eyeball how long the piece should be and when to create the border. I have now made her two new wraps and am working on her third.

Ever since I was a young boy, I've been interested in threadwork, even though nobody in my life ever knitted or was involved in any fiber arts. I started with cross-stitch work in middle school. I enjoyed a few projects, but I never really kept up with it, and by high school, I'd dropped it. Now I know that I will continue to use knitting as a base to develop into a fiber artist. I am thinking about starting to spin and dye my own yarn. I would like to eventually do the whole process, taking the wool from its raw state and working with it until it is knitted into its finished project. I've also met some people who are weavers, and I am looking into getting a loom someday in the future. I never really thought I would take this road, and I would have laughed a few years ago if someone had suggested to me that I could be an artist of any kind.

Almost all my experiences as a male knitter have been positive. I think one reason is that no one who might have issues with it has ever gotten up the courage to approach me. I know that I am breaking down stereotypes for a lot of people. I can tell, because a number of them have to justify what I am doing by talking about other men who have broken stereotypes. The one I hear the most is: "Well, didn't Rosie Greer do needlepoint?" Although both art forms involve thread, they are not that similar, but it seems to make people feel better to remember that.

Most of the time, though, I think people feel comfortable coming up and talking to me, because I am doing something out of the ordinary (at least for men). Women will usually come up and talk to me about my project, and then they'll tell me about their experiences with knitting. My knitting has allowed me to meet so many more people than if I had just been reading a book. Overall, though, I feel that when people see me knitting, I am helping to challenge how male roles are perceived. I am a large man, and due to my balding head, beard, and the fact that I ride a motorcycle, more people assume I am in a biker gang than in a knitting circle. But then they see me knitting, and they realize that they haven't seen men knit before. Then I think they realize that they have always assumed that knitting was something women did. Yet here I am, knitting away.

I love to knit for friends, and I really enjoy it when they wear things I created for them. I will take a friend to the store with me and have them choose the yarn they like. Sometimes that part is a challenge for me, because I am very tactile when it comes to yarn, and they sometimes choose yarns that won't be nice to touch. We discuss what they want and what it will look like, then usually I choose a pattern to create the type of garment they are looking for. I get excited as I think of them wearing it and how much they will enjoy it. I like to have a pattern to fall back on, but I usually adapt it: I want to change the color or lengthen or shorten a certain section. I am just starting to create my own patterns— nothing fancy—for simple sweaters and scarves. It's exciting, because I know that creating my own pattern makes it unique. But I'm still not confident about my skills in this area.

When I am knitting just to knit, and not to give something away, my joy starts with a trip to the yarn store. I will look over the yarns and find the ones I like. This is really the best part for me; I love to feel and touch the various yarns. I love yarns that are soft and silky to the touch, but I also enjoy yarns that are unique (with metal woven in or that just have a completely different look about them). I also really like yarns with deep, rich colors. Unfortunately, the yarns I like best tend to be the most expensive; scarves can cost more than $100 to make, a sweater more than $300. I have to watch myself.

At Artfibers, the knitting store I am now most connected to, there are always pieces hanging in the shop that get me very excited to take on a new project. Some of them are knitted mosaics. I would like to learn how to take dissimilar yarns and create a tapestry I could display. I really love rich, vibrant yarns, yarns that have great texture and feeling, but they aren't really yarns I would ever use to make clothing for myself—they are just not my style. I also love getting to learn new patterns and stitches, and I try to integrate something new into every project. Knitting is a process, and I am always learning new things. I think knitting is a life-long process, not a goal that I will eventually reach.

Not That Kind of Knitter

When the Spirit of man retires to rest, he takes with him materials from this all-containing world, and he creates and destroys his own glory and radiance. Then the spirit of man shines in his own light.

In that land there are no chariots, no teams of horses, nor roads; but he creates his own chariots, his teams of horses, and roads. There are no joys in that region, and no pleasures nor delights; but he creates his own joys, his own pleasures and delights. In that land there are no lakes, no lotus-ponds, nor streams; but he creates his own lakes, his lotus-ponds, and streams. For the Spirit of man is Creator.

—THE UPANISHADS

The more I listened to knitters talk about how they knit and why, the more I felt inclined to analyze my own tendencies. Partly, I think, this was just a natural, progressive by-product of the interviewing process; discussing the habits of others leads you to dissect your own. But the knitters I spoke to also often asked questions of me: What did I knit? When did I start? How? I soon felt that I was not so much interviewing people as just sitting down with them for a good, long talk. And talk about knitting, more often than not, led to talk of extremely personal details about people's lives. "How you do anything is how you do everything," Melanie Loew said the morning I visited Artfibers, and many knitters I spoke to seemed to grasp this idea on a very deep level. I often came away from an hours-long discussion with one newly met knitter, or group of knitters, feeling as though we had experienced a brief but intense period of intimacy. It seemed only fair that I should be willing to share with them something of my own experience.

So what kind of knitter am I? Meticulous, detail-oriented, slightly neurotic, slightly sloppy, driven by research—this I'd already established. But unlike many knitters I met, it became clear to me as the weeks and months progressed that knitting does not dredge up for me any extreme emotional issues. Yes, there were those first few (disturbing) days right after I'd taken up knitting, when in every aspect of the act I seemed to be imitating the habits and facial expressions of my mother, but that had worn off quickly enough. For me, knitting is no guilt assuager, as it is for Dinna and Mitzi, who hate to be idle; no device for dealing with woes; no escape from unhappy details of my life. I knit purely because I like to create, anything at all.

On the five-hour trip I took from Los Angeles to San Francisco, with my husband at the wheel of our rental car, I also discovered this: I am not the kind of pass-the-time knitter who likes to knit in the car. We drove north along the Pacific Coast Highway, a precipitous, mist-blown squiggle of road that hugs cliffs and spectacular oceanfront—but I don't think it was the scenery that brought about my ambivalence for knitting just then. If how I knit is how I do everything, *where* I knit must also fit into this equation.

I like to knit in some of the very same spots I like to read: curled up on my couch with my cat tucked into my lap; snuggled into bed, fighting sleep. As for the car, I've loved to travel this way since I was a small girl, always loved to gaze out the window at even uninspired scenery and imagine myself in a new place, as a new person; I've always half-dreaded arrival and the end of a journey that's inspired such reverie. It's no different now that I'm an adult. The only thing I like to do in the car is ride in the car.

Out of the car, though, tired and brain-frazzled, with my feet set firmly on San Francisco pavement, the only thing I wanted to do was knit. What stopped me? I'd grown tired of my yarn.

7·

A Bridge to Maine

I came home to New York and began transcribing my California interviews. A couple weeks into it, I transcribed the one I'd saved for last, two tapes long, of the L.A. Church of Crafters. No sooner had I finished than I heard the asthmatic rattle of the UPS truck pulling up to the curb, and then my doorbell rang: a package from Hilda Erb. It contained my very own "Stitch 'n' Bitch Los Angeles" bag, neatly folded and wrapped in tissue. It had been sturdily seamed by Hilda from a sheer pink-and-white flowered curtain following an old pattern: the square, wide-strapped style favored by Tibetan Buddhist monks. In it, all summer, I proudly toted my growing pile of swatches, yarn, and needles from one interview and shop visit to the next.

I also started to write back and forth with Vickie, who e-mailed me every once in a while to update me on what was going on in her life (and her knitting) back in L.A. June 10: "I had a very Zen knitting moment yesterday that made me think of you. I'm taking this hardcore self-defense course. During the last class, after a particularly rough fight, I found myself daydreaming about knitting. All I wanted to do was go to a yarn store and find the softest yarn possible to work with." June 26: "I was talking with my narrow-minded Latin father the other day about my SnB group. I was telling him about my friend. Karen is a linguist, a professional, and speaks multiple languages. So my dad says, 'Well it's nice that she'll even come to a group like yours.' Knowing exactly what he meant, of course, I asked, 'What do you mean?' He said, 'Well you know, it's good that she's willing to go someplace and do what you do, and talk about the things you talk about.' 'What do you mean, Dad?' 'You know, women stuff. Aren't those the sorts of things you talk about?' 'Um . . . well, we talk about current events, politics, entertainment, and, oh, I don't know . . . knitting. Yes, Dad, women stuff.'"

Vickie sent me e-mails full of links to knitting sites. Included among them was one maintained by some members of a spinning and knitting group way, way up north (or "downeast," as the locals say) in Ellsworth, Maine. The main focus of the site was a calendar, proceeds of which fund breast cancer research, which featured some of the women romping through the snow; walking for the woods, looms in hand, in dwindling sunlight; sitting on their weathered wood porches—either entirely in the nude or wearing some nevertheless revealing item of their own knitted clothing. The pictures were lovely and funny, and the women looked rugged and decidedly nonurban—worlds away from the Angelinos and New Yorkers I'd been interviewing so far. I ordered myself a copy of the calendar, which arrived with a tuft of creamy fleece, tightly curled at one end, taped to its cover. Inside, in addition to photos of the pinups, were spinning tips and dyeing instructions, and patterns for top-down sweaters and fishermen's vests and—almost best of all—recipes for soup (every spinning meeting revolves not only around spinning, but soup-sipping as well). There were recipes for borscht and minestrone and corn chowder and "nasty rooster soup," the instructions of which begin, earthily enough: "When you find yourself with too many roosters in your flock, choose a few of the meanest. Send their spirits to rooster heaven, pluck, clean, and cut the meat into pieces. . . ."

Almost immediately upon receiving my calendar—something about the whole package made me suddenly long to give up city living for good and head for more rural climes—I contacted the website's spokesperson, who put me in contact with Geri Valentine.

Geri not only spins and dyes her own wool for knitting, but she also shears the sheep for her raw fleece as well. In response to an e-mail query, Geri sent me a twelve-page, handwritten letter—languid, thoughtful, rich with her reminiscences—by snail mail, such an incredibly luxurious undertaking in these speedy Internet days. It arrived in an envelope thick with photographs of Geri's intricate, fantastical socks and sweaters, all one of a kind and bursting with color. I sat for almost an hour at my kitchen table, letter in hand, occasionally reading aloud to my husband, my dog, my cat—or anyone who seemed to be listening— a passage that moved me to the point that I could not keep it to myself.

GERI VALENTINE

. . . [K]nitting has the potential to create magic in our lives.
—KAFFE FASSETT,
GLORIOUS KNITS, 1985

I first learned to knit as a child, at the age of eight or nine, from my Auntie Ben, a next-door neighbor in Duluth, Minnesota, who was not my aunt personally, but she was the auntie to all the children in the neighborhood. She was tall, thin, and white-haired, and she would quiver periodically as if in the beginnings of Parkinson's disease, especially her head. She was a Norwegian woman, a widow, who always told us girls to "never marry a man older than you." She knit lovely, multicolored snowflake mittens with idiot strings for all the kids who lived nearby. She had a half-dozen Siamese cats and made her own elderberry wine, which she would give to us in tiny stemmed glasses. It was sweet and good. I suspect I was eager to learn knitting from her. I remember loving it, finding it easy. My first actual project (after just knitting squares for practice) was a scarf: a long, garter-stitch scarf with fringe at the ends.

I dropped knitting in high school—uncool, I guess—and then picked up crocheting the winter after I graduated in 1971. Crocheting and macramé were big at that time. I kept up with crocheting and some knitting (mostly making shawls and afghans for family Christmas presents) until I learned how to spin my own yarn in 1976. Duluth had—and still has—a spinning and weaving guild that offered classes. When I learned to spin, my needlework changed. I crocheted a rug, a poncho; I began dyeing with lichens and flowers and bark. I remember making a vest out of handspun that was so awesome that I could hardly wear it because when people asked me about it I would blush and become tongue-tied with embarrassment, because I was so *proud* of it.

About this time, I read somewhere that knitting used less yarn than crochet and was less heavy. Homespun can be bulky, especially when one first learns, so I thought knitting might suit my homespun yarn better than crochet. I began knitting sweaters and socks and mittens. In the mid-1980s, I discovered Kaffe Fassett and quietly went berserk, getting into synthetic dyes and bursting into color knitting. That is where I've leveled out with my knitting. Although now, since 1999, I've been returning to vegetable dyes, both gathered in the wild and grown in my garden.

How I think of knitting, and the possibility of it, has only changed in my level of confidence. I loved knitting when I first began, and I love it now; the possibilities of it seemed endless as a beginner, and they seem endless now. I could knit every article of clothing and household cloth if I wanted to, but I don't want to. One could knit a bridge if the fiber were steel and the needles (and knitter) were big enough. Getting better doesn't matter to me if I define getting better as going to school or study-ing the craft. Getting better sounds more fun and interesting if it means losing my fear of failure and enjoying experimenting with new stitches and designs.

I knit for sale and for myself and for gifts for others. It's always harder to knit for others: Will they like it? Will it fit? Will they think it costs too much? Will they think it's horrible and ugly but have to take it, because it's a present? There is sometimes a hesitancy in knitting for others. If I knit on consignment (only someone who loves it will buy it) or for myself, the feeling is freer, more spontaneous.

I knit because I'm a knitter. I knit because I love the ritual of it: selecting a needle (I use round needles, or a set of four for socks or mittens), arraying all my color choices around me, imagining who the knit item will be for. I knit because I love the feel of the whole process: the yarn slipping through my fingers, the vibration of the colors, the slick steel of needle and the soft sounds the needle and yarn make. Spinning is the same. All of the senses are tickled in the process. Homespun wool smells wonderful.

Often, knitting has a calming influence on me, especially when I knit a simple project like socks with only a few colors. When I knit a complicated color pattern, my level of concentration is intense, and some tension in the body comes with that. I don't tend to pick up knitting when I'm stressed or sad. Instead, I go for a walk, hide in a book, or have a nap, or do some yoga or meditation to get a closer look at what's up for me. I think I knit more often when I'm feeling positive and optimistic. I certainly pick up my knitting (or pull up the spinning wheel) if a phone conversation drags on or if I have to ride in a car or bus or attend a boring meeting.

I suspect my color choices are affected by my moods. It certainly isn't something I *think* much about; rather, I reach for the color more by instinct. The mind has little to do with it during the knitting process. Outside influences affect what I knit in practical ways, such as choosing socks or mittens while riding in a car because they are small projects, or choosing a less complicated pattern to knit while at a meeting because of distractions.

The joy of knitting first begins when I desire the object of clothing in my mind. I *want* a coat. I *want* a pair of mittens to give to a friend for her birthday. For me, the process also begins when I shear a sheep and see the white (or gray or brown) rolls of fresh wool peel away from the animal. Especially if there is luster to the wool, I begin to imagine how the luster will shine through the dyed color, adding extra light to the yarn and to the knitting. I really enjoy all the processes of knitting: shearing; spinning; dyeing; planning the garment, including the swatch, if needed, and any chartwork for color design; casting on the chosen needle; knitting; sewing the garment together; choosing buttons and sewing them and the label on; washing and blocking. I think the deepest joy of knitting is in the thick of it: sitting with my color palette arrayed around me and feeling and watching the pattern evolve.

I design my own patterns. My original sock and mitten patterns were from books, and my first sweater was a pattern. I quickly found that homespun yarn doesn't translate to patterns well. For a coat or a color pattern I've never actually knit before, I often will use chart paper to work out the multiples for an inch or so. Once the repetitions start making sense, I drop the chart. Most of my color choices are spontaneous, evolving during the knitting process, and for large areas of background color, I make "patterns in blue" or "patterns in purple," off the cuff. This is really fun.

I live in the woods and grow vegetables and flowers; I think color in nature influences me a lot, the way the purple rhododendron blossom sets off the green leaf, and the shade and sun dappling the green leaf brings in depth and interest. Kaffe Fassett's *Glorious Knits* was a major inspiration for me. I had just begun dyeing lots of colors, and crocheting and knitting purses and socks, and his book sent me deeply into color knitting, and his patterns were a visual inspiration for many of my first items of clothing. Through his book, I learned the intarsia method of carrying color, which is a central technique for me. I also learned the knitting in of ends, a method of doing the finishing work that saves endless hours of work once the garment is finished.

There have been times, while knitting intricate color patterns, when my concentration has been as focused as during meditation. Hours have gone by, dusk has fallen, and I'm too intent on my work to rise and light a lamp. There are similarities for me between knitting and meditation, and maybe even a link. I found meditation to be very pleasant, even easy, from the beginning. Maybe the ability to sit and focus was first learned with the knitting process.

I've belonged to my spinning group for twenty-two years. I worked on a sheep farm in southern Maine, and I delivered a ram lamb to a downeast farm that belonged to Cynthia Thayer, a member of the spinning group. I eventually moved downeast, and I took Cynthia up on her offer to join the group. The importance of spinning my own wool is major for me. When I learned to spin and made that first handspun, hand-dyed vest that I mentioned earlier, I tapped into a well of self-satisfaction and authenticity that I really needed in my life. The act of learning to spin propelled me out of a dead marriage, out of Minnesota, and up to Maine to work on the sheep farm. I was, as Joseph Campbell says, following my bliss.

Shearing sheep ties into this "do it from scratch" need I have. It's an important facet of who I am. I am just completing my own log cabin, which I built myself with the help of two friends. I've been working on this house since 1999, when we cut the trees. The foundation is made of scavenged stone from local granite quarries. It's beautiful, this house. It's me. Like my knitting, it's my life force manifesting.

I share my raw wool with others and occasionally sell fleeces, which are whole clips from one animal. I shear at more than 100 farms in three counties in Maine each spring, and I get paid per animal. I also shear on three offshore islands (Nash, Little Nash, and Flat Islands off South Addison, northeast of Mt. Desert Island), where there are more than 200 sheep. I take my shearing pay in wool. It's beautiful, clean, strong wool with a lot of luster. I always have too much to spin, and I don't like to keep it around for more than a year or two because of moths. So I give a lot away, especially to a friend who teaches spinning and to new spinners, who do well to start with beautiful wool so the frustration of learning is lessened.

As I mentioned, I dye my own yarn. I use synthetic dyes—Ciba Kiton, Cushing—and natural dyes. My sister sends me black walnut hulls from Iowa. I grow madder root (orange and red) in my garden, and Japanese indigo (blue). I harvest goldenrod from local fields. I collect onion skins from my cooking all winter and dye with those. I use poplar, birch, and alder bark from the trees and shrubs on the 230 acres I live on with two friends.

I'm a knitter who uses knitting as a vehicle for creativity, for the expression of my imagination. Being practical, I love making things I can use, like sweaters, socks, mittens, coats, and rugs (and I also weave). I think of Pablo Neruda's poem "Ode to a pair of socks," which I've received from friends who think of me when they read it. It's the story of a pair of socks that are so beautiful, so genuine, that the wearer can barely stand to put them on his feet. The outcome is that the joy of warm feet in winter is a double joy when the warmth is beautiful.

Art and craft come together in knitting for me, and the pleasure of using the finished items daily in my home and on my body brings deep satisfaction. I know where this pair of socks comes from, intimately.

More Yarn

[L]et one, observing solitude which is not pleasing to others, walk alone like a rhinoceros.

—Khaggavisana Sutra (Rhinoceros Discourse)

Since I'd grown sick of my yarn, there was clearly only one thing to do about it: buy more. Luckily, this is an easy enough prospect when you are spending your days in knitting shops, surrounded by balls and skeins of every imaginable specification. At Artfibers in San Francisco, I browsed and wandered the aisles, contemplating the vast and unique selection until I was able to settle on two balls: one, called Altamira, a variegated red-and-yellow blend of ultra mohair/cotton/nylon spun into a curly, "naturally elastic strand." The other, Kyoto, was a silk-based wool/mohair blend in a deep red reminiscent of Tibetan monks' robes, with a slight metallic sheen. I also bought one skein from Mel at Wildfiber: a bumpy, variegated Eisaku Noro wool in shades of green and eggplant and bark. And I bought two balls from Edith at La Knitterie Parisienne: a tiny-gauge kid mohair in the palest blue, and a slightly thicker, fuzzier blend of medium-gauge pond blue toned with the humid green of a late-afternoon thunderstorm.

While I was still visiting San Francisco, I knit one swatch, with Kyoto, called Bells and Bell-Ropes. It turned out looking only marginally like its picture, which showed a very pretty up-and-down pattern of tight, curvaceous bells strung together on narrow pulls. I suppose it was a success. I only had to pull out one row, while my hostess—by her own admission, not a "crafty" type—poured me a glass of wine and then stood by my shoulder to witness the unraveling; and the only mistake was a small hole near the cast-off, made when my hostess refilled my wine glass, then came to sit next to me to ask things like, "What are you doing?" and "What are you doing now?"

I didn't knit a single other swatch for all the rest of my time in California.

I told myself I was too busy, too tired, too hot to want to knit. That was assuredly part of it—long days spent driving around and conducting interviews and socializing, most of them in sunny, sweaty conditions. I told myself that I was irritated with the inherent foibles of swatching—losing my count, losing my patience, pictures in the book looking bigger, smaller, neater, better than my own squares. But I think I was irritated, most of all, by that condition that plagues legions of houseguests: lack of solitude. (My husband likes to quote a Russian proverb: *"V goste khorosho, doma lusha"*. "As a guest is good, but home is better.") And if there was one reality this condition was forcing me to confront, it was that I am, most decidedly, a person who likes to knit *alone*.

8.

A (Virtual) Visit to Ithaca

You *must* meet my friend Joey." So commanded one of my best (non-knitting) friends, Pankti, who had worked with Joey (Josephine) Cardamome for several years at the Alternative Community School in Ithaca, New York. "She has a wonderful heart," said Pankti, "and she's a rare individual who can genuinely understand middle- and high school thinking. Oh, and she's an awesome knitter."

Originally, I'd hoped to meet Joey, to drive up to Ithaca for at least a brief tête-à-tête. I was feeling somewhat cut off from certain knitters—those who lived in places I'd been unable visit, like Chicago and New Mexico and Maine—deprived of a face to attach to words and of an up-close look at knitting projects I'd come to know only through detailed descriptions. But the summer plodded along, and schedules filled up (Joey's daughter was getting married), and despite my best intentions, I was never able to manage a trip to Ithaca.

Most fortunately for me, Joey proved a dedicated correspondent. The first of her communiqués was so laden with intricacies and insights that I wrote to her again to ask her to elaborate. She responded with even more compelling details, and so I wrote back to her again, and then again, and again. And each time she answered, it seemed, she offered another piece of herself.

JOEY CARDAMOME

[A]ll praise to that art which can assuage a sorrow or lighten an affliction.

—MRS. WARREN & MRS. PULLAN,

TREASURES IN NEEDLEWORK, 1855

I think my mother taught me to knit, but I don't remember it. She had ten kids—I was number two—and was pretty busy and only knit a little bit herself. I knit sporadically during my childhood, mainly scarves, nothing too fancy. No one else in my family knits now: none of my six sisters, nor my mom, nor my dad or three brothers. Most of my sisters did knit as teens, usually something for a boyfriend, such as mittens. But often, the relationship would break up soon after, so our family has a joke about not knitting anything for a boyfriend. My whole family thinks I'm some kind of wonder since I can knit a sweater.

I really started seriously knitting once I was single again and my kids were teens or older. I began making sweaters for them out of thick lopi wool and liked the way they looked. We have a very good yarn store in Ithaca. The owner specializes in quality yarns—no acrylics—and she provides a lot of help when knitters get stuck. Generally, my knitting is much too loose and I have to use smaller needles to make the garment right. But a few years ago, during a crisis, I knit a sweater and it was much too small because I had tightened up due to anxiety.

When my husband and I were breaking up, twenty years ago, I was knitting a white sweater for no one in particular; I half thought of giving it to our therapist. She was a pastoral counselor and wasn't charging us anything, even though she was seeing us very often. I was feeling so abandoned and hurt and lied to, and I trusted her caring for me. I guess she was a life preserver I was clinging to, and I wanted to give her something for her own comfort. Anyway, I kept making serious mistakes in the sweater and needed to undo all the work and start again. This happened a lot of times and I compared myself to Odysseus's wife, Penelope, who fooled her suitors by telling them she would choose one of them when her weaving of a shroud for her father-in-law, Laertes, was finished; then she worked on it during the day and ripped it out at night.* Since then, I think of knitting (and life) in metaphoric terms.

In the last ten years, I have knit an adult sweater every year. A lot of times, it is for a person who needs comfort due to tragedy or other stresses. I usually get a sense of who needs a sweater and then approach them. We go to the store to pick out the wool (I buy it; it has to be a total gift). It's funny how hard it is for some people to have that much attention paid to them and how they can't decide on the colors. I tell them

*"Thereafter in the daytime I would weave at my great loom, but in the night I would have torches set by, and undo it so for three years I was secret in my designs, convincing the Achaians, but when the fourth year came with the seasons returning, and the months faded, and many days had been brought to completion, then at last through my maidservants, those careless hussies, they learned, and came upon me and caught me, and gave me a scolding. So, against my will and by force, I had to finish it."

I am knitting a prayer into every stitch to protect them—just like King Arthur's half sister, Morgaine, who embroidered a rune into every stitch of the tunic she made for him to wear into battle.

It's important to me that the recipients of my sweaters be around for as much of the knitting as possible. I like for them to be part of the experience, because they're nurtured and calmed by watching the needles. It's not always possible, but it makes me feel gratified when they can see how much love and work goes into the thousands of knots. One friend watched and got nervous, because he's a perfectionist and I'm very casual. I drop stitches and laugh and try to find them; I have to take out many rows to find where I made a mistake; a lot of times, I'll leave the sweater on the floor when I'm not knitting. But the thing is, the sweater always comes out beautifully.

I make these sweaters for people I know, very intimate friends. One was a young woman who had been my student. She is wonderful and smart and deep, but initially I did not know her very well. I was quite close with her brother, who was also a sublime human. He was killed in a car accident, and the young woman and I spent a lot of time together those first horrible weeks after. I was the first person she called when the police came to her house to tell her the news. About two months after he died, I knew I wanted to make her a sweater. We went and picked out the wool, which was hard because she's not into fashion or thinking about colors. It comforted me to make her a sweater to help protect her in this life without her brother; he was her only sibling, and they had an absolutely incredible love between them. So some of my own grief was assuaged by caring for her in that way. Since then, she and I have become very close and important people in each other's lives.

I actually have one style of sweater, which I make pretty regularly. I know how to do it, and it looks very good, so I stick with it. It usually has one main color, all knit on circular needles with lopi wool (which still has the sheep's lanolin in it, so it feels good while you work it). Then I do a pretty cool design of two or three other colors starting at the waist and cuff, just above the ribbed part, that goes across the chest, over the arm, across the back, and around the other arm. Often, for a child, I'll knit their name into the chest part, then do little people holding hands (à la dolls cut from newspaper) across the back. I have also made replicas of the one sweater I sort of remember that my mom made for the oldest kid in our family. My mom is a packrat and still has the pattern she used in 1952. Two of my nephews have gotten that one.

One person picked a more complicated pattern, which was a challenge for me. That's the one I was making when the entire sweater was too small. People suggested that I just give it to a smaller person, but when I'm making a sweater, I really am trying to put prayers for that particular person into it. So I had to rip it out and do it over. Since then, I have unfortunately done a lot more ripping out than I used to. I'm afraid it's a pattern now. But I also see it as I'm going through big changes in my own psyche. I tend to be reflective and serious. I think these past few years—I turned fifty three years ago—I have been trying very hard to change how I relate to the world and to let go of some lifelong defense mechanisms. I guess the ripping out and reknitting is a metaphor for me trying to change and having to repeat the lessons a lot—you can't just be different the first time you try. It actually doesn't bother me as much as people think it will. I like the process of knitting as much as the product. I also like to see how much it calms children and adults just to watch me knit.

At the public, alternative secondary school where I teach English and ESL, one whole day a week is devoted to projects that are divided into four slots. One year, during one of the slots, I offered a knitting class. Fortunately, a few good knitters came who could help the non-knitters, because I am not great at teaching this skill. So we sat around and knit. It was actually more for the socialization than for the knitting education. The students were sixth- to twelfth-graders, male and female. The next semester, we limited it to high-schoolers and called it "Knitting and Dreaming," because we shared our dreams during the project. Then two seniors not participating in the knitting project each decided to make a sweater for their senior project (it's a requirement for all seniors to complete a thirty-hour project on something they wanted to learn that they hadn't had a chance to yet). The senior boy, Dylan, had knit a little as an elementary student at a Waldorf school but had forgotten how to do it. I showed him the basic knit stitch and thought he would practice for a while, but he just started a sweater on round needles with no pattern. He ended up making an extraordinary sweater with all kinds of designs in different colors, and it fit just right. He seemed to do it naturally, with virtually no help.

The female student, Becca, was similarly amazing. She knit a rectangle for the front on straight needles, and then left a hole for her head and knit down the back side of the sweater. She made sleeves and put it together, and it was also a beautiful sweater. Neither of them used patterns. They went against all the wisdom of knitting (impossible for most of us to do and still produce a recognizable sweater), and they each had a sense of how to make it work. Anytime I deviate from a pattern, the piece ends up looking ridiculous. They were a lot more confident than I am. I thought they were magicians.

Knitting fulfills a lot of needs for me: to be busy when sitting, to have a way to detach from the social scene by focusing on the knitting, to connect deeply with a person by giving him or her a gift, to feel creative and productive. I am intrigued by the way making knots with string can create a piece of clothing. Also, knitting can be a way to connect with people in other situations. Many times it is a conversation starter. I went to China a year and a half ago to accompany my sister, who was adopting a baby. There were thirteen families in our group, and we had a tour bus and a guide. We stayed in Hong Kong and then in two cities in mainland China. The rest of the group only wanted to leave the hotel in the tour bus, but I liked to go out and walk around in the city. I had a small language book so I could point to the English words: "I am American" or "I am a teacher." The person would look where I was pointing and see the translation in Chinese characters, and he or she would smile and nod. Usually, a group would gather and we would laugh and nod at one another. Many women passed the time in the market or on the sidewalk by knitting, so I walked up to two of them and pantomimed knitting. They smiled—all the people I met were tickled by any attention—so I mimed that I wanted to show them that I could knit and one of them handed me her work. It was a purple sweater for a kid. I knit a few stitches. That drew a crowd of very excited people.

The next day, and the days after that, I brought my own knitting when I went out. At the time, I was knitting a sweater for the sister I was traveling with. She always wanted her own family but never had a relationship that led to that. She was in her forties and taking the plunge to adopt, and she was really scared. I would sit next to the women and knit alongside them. People would gather around us to watch. I even have a photo of me and a serious-looking woman knitting at her butcher kiosk.

I'm a knitter who isn't good at much that is creative. I was always en-
vious of people who could putter at their craft or hobby (auto mechan-
ics, playing guitar, painting, designing model airplanes or clothing, or
whatever). I do take piano lessons and practice a lot, but I never allowed
myself to think either that or the knitting was creative, because I need to
play piano pieces composed by other people, and I knit sweaters from
patterns. If I didn't work from patterns, the pieces would fit a giraffe/
elephant/squirrel mix. But now I think those two hobbies really *are* my
creative outlet. The piano playing is just for me. The knitting is for other
people—it's a way to demonstrate my nurturing and love for someone.
And it makes me feel quite useful when I otherwise might feel lazy just
sitting around. The whole process still feels a little like magic to me.

Back to Brooklyn

Feel the fine qualities of creativity permeating your breast and assuming
delicate configurations.

—Shiva to Devi, "Centering," *Vigyan Bhairava, Sochanda*
Tantra, Malini Vijaya Tantra

Back home to Brooklyn, at very long last. Thinking I was ready to
knit again, I lined up all the balls and skeins that I'd bought on my
trip, along with the remains of their predecessors, on a large, low table in
my living room, waiting to be touched by the knitting muses. For a long

while, though, I felt inclined to do precisely nothing with the yarn—nothing, that is, but stare at it.

I cannot exactly pinpoint what occurred to bring on my inertia, or finally to banish it. Maybe the sultry, stultifying heat of July in New York dropped an increment or two; maybe the daily acts of reading about knitting, and writing about knitting, triggered in my brain a remorse for my slothfulness; maybe it was as simple as, "Sometimes I feel like it, sometimes I don't." At any rate, I emerged from what felt like a long knitting drought ready to return to swatching but determined to be done with the knit-purl combinations and fancy texture patterns I'd so far been favoring. What I wanted now was a real challenge.

I found a picture of Persian Lace that reminded me of the filigree windows that are painstakingly chiseled out of the stucco walls of buildings in the westerly Indian region of Rajasthan, where I'd once traveled. To knit it, I chose the blue-green mohair blend I'd picked up at Edith's, a substantial enough yarn, I thought, to really show off the pattern. Of course—I was no longer surprised by this anomaly—the pattern proved to be larger than its picture implied, but for once, I didn't mind. Its ornate, rounded diamond shapes lying side by side on a field of garter stitch was stunning, especially when held up to the light, or a white wall, or my own skin in order to better see the stitches. Wrapping the swatch around my wrist, then walking to the mirror and wrapping it again, around my neck, I began for the first time to consider some potential use for my swatches: cuff, turtleneck, hat brim, blanket hem, sock top. It was no longer the infinite variety of swatching, but the possibilities of patterns and shapes and colors and gauges, combined with potential applications, that was now beginning to intrigue me.

9 ·

Twisted Diary and Into the
Desolate Wilds

Before Tina Marrin and Suzan Mischer of L.A.'s Knit Café ever became acquainted, each of them, separately, coincidentally, met the Twisted Sisters at a knitting convention in Riverside, California. And it was the two of them who good-naturedly insisted that I contact the Sisters, a trio of San Diego women who are not sisters but friends, and in their non-knitting lives, serious professionals: Anna Walden is a psychotherapist, Terri Cupurdijo is co-owner of a company that wires buildings for computer communications, and Barbara Levin is Associate Vice President of Investments for Prudential Financial. As the Twisted Sisters, though, they hand-paint luxury fibers to sell to select shops across the country and also design garments to sell in kits with their yarns and patterns.

Anna, who, unusually enough, learned to knit as a child on "unraveled soakers that my mother made for me during World War II," told me that the contributions of the Twisted Sisters "overlap considerably. Mine is designing garments, dying, and in particular, mixing color, which

I love. My specific area for the business is education: organizing, writing, and often teaching classes." Barbara does all the pattern editing and publishing, sees to most of the contact with yarn shop owners and generally does "a little bit of everything, except figure out dye formulas, which is Terri's bailiwick." As I struggled to knit up even one error-free swatch in a whole, long evening, I wondered, most of all, where they found the time.

BARBARA LEVIN

We are but skirmishers on the out-posts, experimentalists in the fam-ily parlour.

—MRS. HOPE,
THE KNITTER'S CASKET, 1898

Twisted Sisters came to be on a long drive back from a three-day private dyeing workshop by Kathryn Alexander (see page 223), which I organized three or four years ago for eight people at my brother's vacation home in Lake Tahoe. I'm still convinced it was oxygen deprivation that did it. We were driving at about 7,000 feet—a pretty high altitude for us sea-level dwellers—when we started kicking around ideas. I asked, "What should we do with all this knowledge now? How do we get into the knitting business?"

During the workshop, we dyed energized yarn the first day, and we knit with it for the next two days. We each dyed about a pound of yarn (enough for a sweater) and wound it into those tiny skeins Kathryn uses. You can imagine that with eight of us dyeing that much yarn at once, we had quite a production line going across the back deck. Kathryn's so-called "energized yarn" has to be kept under tension as it dries, and that was quite a scene. We used everything we could find to hang yarn from. I remember we took all the logs out of the firewood holder, turned the holder upside down, and had yarn hanging from that. We used large soda bottles full of water, and fireplace logs, and anything else we could find.

It was such a treat to have Kathryn to ourselves for three days. We were so enthused about her that the first dyeing we attempted after the Tahoe trip was on six pounds of energized yarn. We did this in Terri's backyard. Her husband bolted some steel bars to the back porch columns, and we hung dozens of mini-skeins from them and anchored them to the lower bar using bungee cords. We had so much tension on those bars that they bent. We were worried they might launch them-selves into space and knock out aircraft. It was a relief the next morning to find that the porch was still standing.

Knitting is something I do all the time, regardless of mood. I don't know whether you could call it a habit or an actual physical addiction, but I knit virtually every day and *have* to have my knitting along when I travel (even though I may not touch it during the trip). I've taken knitting on whitewater rafting and camping trips. I've sat by a pool in Maui swatch-ing alpaca and wool (OK, it was in the shade). The only time it's not a joy is when I'm trying a new design and it's not working out the way I want it to. But then I shift into figuring out how to save the project without rip-ping out (thank God for creative partners), and that becomes fun, too.

I learned to knit when I was about seven or eight years old. For some reason, it was the "in" thing that summer at the swim club my family belonged to. During the adults-only swim breaks (ten minutes of each hour), we girls would sit and knit. Our normal swim-break activity was to play jacks, using our dads' old golf balls and Formica slabs cut out from leftovers of kitchen countertops. We were really proficient at jacks and could all get up into the fivesies and sixies—you get a great bounce with a golf ball on Formica—and that summer we alternated between playing jacks and knitting. I still have the first thing I knit: a pink wool scarf with the edges seamed together for about six inches to make an attached hood. I recall knitting something out of an aqua yarn with some glitter in it (very 1950s) and a yellow wool sweater. My first go-around with knitting may have lasted a year or two.

A friend of my mother's, Dora Sack, taught me. She lived about three blocks from our house, and I remember hopping on my bicycle with my knitting in the bike basket and racing over there every time I had a knitting catastrophe (riding without a helmet and with straight metal needles; these days my mother would be arrested for allowing that kind of behavior). She was a spectacular knitter—I seem to remember her working on a Chanel-style suit—and very patient.

I started up again when I was first married. My now-ex-husband loved to go to the horse track, and I was bored just sitting there. It was too distracting to try to read, so I started knitting again. Interesting, now that I recall: my first project was pink (more of a mauve, actually), and I am definitely not a person who wears pink. Anyway, anything knit at the track had to be thoroughly washed or dry-cleaned to get the tobacco smoke out of it. The Meadowlands was especially bad for smoke odors.

I knit a scarf for my fiancé for a birthday present last winter. Not only hasn't he ever had the chance to wear it, he hasn't seen it for months (it's been "on tour" with the Twisted Sisters at various knitting shows and conventions), and he claims not to remember what it looks like. Now that I'm in the knitting business, about the only thing I've been knitting for family and friends lately are baby clothes—but only one item per family. The second baby gets something from The Gap.

Because of Twisted Sisters, I design my own patterns or knit samples of my partners' designs. This makes it extremely difficult to go into a yarn store—I know I can't buy yarn, because I have no time to knit it, and there are so many designers out there whose patterns I'd love to try, and there are so many beautiful yarns. Terri has saved me a few times in various yarn shops by telling me very forcefully that I am not allowed to buy yarn. When we started Twisted Sisters, I had just begun creating sweaters that were free-form, or designed on the needles. That is, I had a template, or outline of the shape of the finished piece, and I would knit in many directions and with many yarns until the piece I was knitting was approximately the size and shape of the template. I don't do that anymore, because it's extremely hard to translate that style into a knitting pattern that other people can follow. So my style of knitting has changed, but my love of (or psychological dependence on) the process has not changed at all.

 Twisted Sister Anna Walden said: "The best knitter I know is Kathryn Alexander. Need I say more? She is an artist, truly innovative and yet a consummate craftsperson." And Barbara Levin, too, was clearly enamored.

What choice did I have? I e-mailed Kathryn at her home in upstate New York, and the same day she wrote back, inviting me to visit: "Just jump on the train and have a wonderful two-hour ride along the scenic Hudson. I will pick you up at the station and drive you back. You would love it; it is beautiful here, and it would be an experience I guarantee would be with you forever! I would even pay half your train fare. Is that spooky? I would fix you a wonderful lunch and you would really understand why I knit."

Again, with a generous offer like that, what choice did I have? Instead of taking the train, though, my husband, Rob, borrowed his grandfather's truck, and the two of us spent a sunny, cool summer Saturday morning driving up the scenic Taconic Parkway. At about noon, we arrived at Kathryn's house—an idyll, pretty much as she described it to me: a shuttered brick house hinged with a newer (c. 1880) addition, of sage-painted wood, and a long porch punctuated by a former smokehouse functioning as Kathryn's temporary studio. A large barn was about to be moved from where it sat, across the road, to perch nearer to the house; this would eventually serve as Kathryn's permanent studio, as well as a gallery to showcase her work and a space in which to conduct workshops.

We pulled into the driveway and Kathryn, who had been sitting on the porch, knitting, walked over to greet us. It was a beautiful day, so we stood on the porch, aimlessly chatting, and after a while we walked over to the knitting Kathryn had left in front of her rocking chair. It was the workings of a sweater, an emerging shape in dozens of colors that would serve as the pattern for a sweater kit—her second. Arrayed around the bit of knitting was part of her palette: fifteen or more colors of fine-gauge, hand-dyed wool fastened to metal binder rings and tagged with dye-lot numbers—"Well, kind of, anyway," says Kathryn. "The numbers have the dye recipes on them that are attached to color cards. I can repeat them, but they will not be identical—thank goodness for that."

Then Kathryn began to lead us slowly through the rooms of her house, which was painted on the inside in surprisingly soothing shades of purple and green and yellow and blue. Every room was scattered with metalwork and furniture made by her husband and Kathryn's own knitting and weaving—tunics and gloves and hats—which hung on racks or was propped on tables and shelves; upstairs, old ski sweaters were tacked up on the walls for decoration, like paintings. We walked through the house, from room to room to room, and then back out to Kathryn's studio. And then, after almost two hours of talking, when we were all famished and parched, she asked, "How about some lunch?" And in her kitchen, with its low windows overlooking a green field, Kathryn toasted tortillas and sautéed vegetables and diced cheese—she was once a fry cook—and blended up her own special recipe for lemonade, spiked with fresh mint.

KATHRYN ALEXANDER

Your sweater should be like your own favorite recipes—like no one else's on earth. And a good thing, too.

—ELIZABETH ZIMMERMANN,
KNITTING WITHOUT TEARS, 1971 (1995)

Part of what makes my work so different is that I'm *creating* the product to *make* the product. My yarn is all handspun, all singles, and it tends to be really fine. I make my own colorways when I dye the yarn. I use tons of color, and it's the way I put those colors together in a piece that makes my work uniquely my own. No one is going to put the same colors together; everyone has their own identity. It's like anything you do; if it's coming from inside you, it's personal. My sweaters aren't something I copy. This can't be repeated by anybody else unless they repeat the piece, and you can tell it's repeated, because it doesn't have my colors, and it's usually made with commercial yarn.

My things have been published for a long time, and a lot of people copy them. I'm not opposed to that at all. If I was breasting all my ideas, it wouldn't be nearly as exciting for me. It's kind of neat to have people copy something I've made—that's part of the fun. There was a point early on where maybe I only had one good idea—that was for my en-trelac sock. It was a new thing that happened in knitting in the early '90s, and it was my first good idea, and I didn't know if I would have any more.

Now that I realize I have new ideas that are forthcoming, I'm not as protective of them as I used to be.

Because my sweaters are so free-form, this is low-stress work for me. If I think about anything in a sweater—and rarely do I think this—I think, *Will it be a cardigan? Will it be something I just pull over?* And that's about as far as I go in planning. I don't usually start knitting until I have about sixty colors dyed. I just pick my favorite color, and then I start in garter stitch. I have to begin somewhere, but I don't know where it's going to be in the sweater. I just knit, and you can trace the thread of my ideas in every sweater.

I have just a few elements that go into every garment: I have tons of color, and I use entrelac shapes, garter stitch, Fair Isle, and I-cord. I rearrange the elements and make a different-shape garment each time. That keeps my interest level high, getting to do something new. That's why these are fun for me, and almost addicting, because each one is like a bunch of little swatches. I never get bored, and if I get stuck in a place that's tough to dig out of because I've made a weird shape, I'll just go and work somewhere else on the piece and come back to it later.

I knit all in one piece. That sweater out there on the porch is all one piece, and I'm on the last arm. I put it together as I go, but I don't sew it together. I knit in every direction to get the thing to stick together. I just hold it up and say, "*Hmm,* that looks long enough." The sweater out there is going to be a kit. Because this is a pattern that I've written text for (which I despise), I have to take all sorts of notes while I'm making it, and I have to measure it; it drives me insane. But my work has been around so long that people are starting to knock it off, so I thought, *I bet-*

ter do these kits before someone else does. I'd like people to know that these are my ideas, and I'd like to get credit for them.

I want people to make my sweaters; they're really easy to make. They're geometric, and they flow together easily. I'm curious to see who changes the kit, which is what I'm hoping will happen—my pattern is just a suggestion. I had a group of six women who live all across the United States buy a kit together. They were a little tentative because they thought it was difficult, which it isn't, but it looks complex. They've set up a support group for themselves online, and they're making it together.

People always ask me, "Where does your inspiration come from?" It comes from my work. It sounds obnoxious, but my work inspires me to do other work, and that's where all my ideas come from. I've already got the idea for my next sweater, and that's because I've been working on the sweater for my next kit. I'm really interested in drape, so I use thinner yarns and a loose gauge. I like to make things wide, because then they can hang, and that way they fit everybody. A silhouette of a body is interesting no matter what size you are, if you don't do weird things to it with underwear.

The reason I knit is because I didn't know how to play pinochle. I was planting trees for Scott Paper in Washington State, and it was wet there, because you plant trees in the winter. I was on an all-male crew— nine stinky guys, their gear, wet wool, sweat, and other things I refused to identify. We would plant trees all morning, and then we would pile into the Crummy—that is, the big rig or Suburban we would drive to the planting site, and it was crummy, let me tell you—and heat it up because we were cold. The men all played cards at noon—pinochle—and I didn't play pinochle, so I would read and listen to their banter. A couple of months later they hired another woman, and she didn't play pinochle either, but she knit, and she sat behind me—you always had to sit in the same place in the Crummy; if you took someone's place, you were really in trouble. And I thought, *Wow, that is a great idea.* I was thinking: work socks. So I asked her if she would teach me to knit during lunch hours.

Spin-Off did a call for entries on socks for their Winter 1992 issue, and I thought, *That'd be cool—maybe mine'll get in there.* They landed on the cover. It was really good timing, because my husband, Mark, and I had moved to Berkeley so he could go to school, and I had just moved into my studio in an old piano factory. Getting on the cover meant I was immediately validated. In Washington, I'd been teaching local people; I was already doing this in a small way. But when I moved to Berkeley, everything changed for me, because I saw so much that I never would have seen in northwest Washington State, even day-to-day things, like how to display flower arrangements and ways to present your work. I went to one exhibit: The whole room was filled with the skeletons of sewn garments—the flat-felt seams of things were hung everywhere. You know how different companies, like Standard Oil, have their own chambray shirts? The artist had hung a whole row of these different chambray shirts, just the flat-felt seams and the collars and the tags behind them. I walked in there and I went, "Wow, that is so amazing; I never would have thought about a garment in that way." I was exposed to new ways of *thinking* about things as much as I was to *seeing* things. I wondered, *What got them to the point at which they thought about that thing in such a new and exciting way?* And I started to bring those ways of thinking to something as humble and traditional as knitting.

I was in the horse industry before knitting, and before that I fought forest fires and planted trees. I was stallion manager at a racetrack farm that did breeding for Thoroughbreds, and it was that job, a particular incident there, that made me go in this direction. It was kind of a risky business. One of the jobs I had to do was show stallions to prospective clients when they decided they wanted to breed their mares. There was one really obnoxious client who would come unannounced every year, in the middle of winter. I had already turned the horses out—the first thing they do is roll in the mud. I was supposed to have three of them out for the client to look at, so I was hurrying to get them cleaned up. I was working on one that was touchy about having his legs brushed; I was in a hurry, so I wasn't giving him the leeway he needed, and he let me know. He was hooked to the wall, and he pulled back and pulled the entire stall wall on him and me. He went down, and I went down. His legs were right on my chest; he could have started scrambling, panicked, but he didn't. I was looking into one of his eyes, and right then I was thinking, *Kathryn, you might want to think about another profession, because I don't think you're going to be doing this when you're sixty.* Right after that, I tried to figure out how I could do my knitting and make a living at it. And right after *that,* we moved to Berkeley. I thought, *Well, I'm already on a roll here—might as well go with this instead of getting some dinky job. Might as well promote myself and my own talents.*

One of the reasons I've succeeded—and I think it's fair to say that I have—is that I did this full-time. All the other artists I knew did something else—they called it "supporting their habit." I never saw it that way; I saw it as a serious business endeavor. Things were really bad at one point in Berkeley—we either had to sell our car or live in our car. We couldn't afford to pay the rent on our house. So we sold our car. We made a lot of decisions like that for me to be able to do this. I've been lucky, but I've also worked really hard and marketed myself. *You* are part of the package. You can make it a bummer, or you can make it kind of cool. This is all I do, my whole life, every waking moment this is what I do, and I'm going to make it fun the whole time, if I can.

I feel like my work is worth seeing—I think it's different enough and exciting enough. People say you can't ever come up with a new idea, everything's already been done. I totally disagree. There are all sorts of ways you can reinvent old work and give it a new twist. I think I'm doing that and people need to see it, because it's going to affect their work somehow. Everything I see that's interesting—like that garment exhibit in Berkeley—I take a little piece of that home with me and incorporate it. When I see something so well-done, it has a huge physical effect on me; I'll never forget it. If I could do that for anyone, ever, I would be so happy.

[Kathryn breezes back through the house, which she's been gently leading me through all along, out across the porch, and into her bright, cheerful studio.]

Teaching was a really good way for me to have a steady income in Berkeley. I could set up a teaching schedule a year in advance and know that I had money coming in. Any money I made selling my work was extra. These days, I'll go out and teach for guilds or conferences: spinning, dying, and knitting. I teach people who have always relied on patterns how to make a sweater that fits their body without using a pattern. Most of the people who come are older women, and I'm reteaching them how to think about their work. I'm going to stop traveling, though, and only teach here. This is an environment that induces work; it makes the work happen in a free-flowing way. My work makes me change my environment, and my environment makes my work change. I'll just be sitting here in my studio, knitting, thinking, *I should paint that door, it looks really bad*. And I'll put my knitting down and paint the door. And then I'll take that and put it back into my knitting. Everything's connected.

I have to be good at a lot of things to make my product—I don't just have to be a creative knitter. I have to know all about fleece and physics, and a lot about chemistry. Initially, I went to conferences and took classes from teachers, but I've learned most of the intricacies on my own, out of curiosity. I really pay attention to what I do. By paying attention to it, I can gain the knowledge to change it. I've been doing research on knit surfaces with energy. When you twist a yarn and spin it, you're adding energy to it, but that energy is usually depleted when you ply it. It gets twisted back in the opposite direction, or it gets washed, if it's a single. But I'm using that energy to create surfaces, making S's and Z's, yarns moving in both directions. I've completely changed knit and purl surfaces to the point that you can't even recognize them. I've always done it in my weaving—it's called "collapsed structures." I thought, *If it works in weaving, I bet it would be* really *interesting in knitting*.

I've never been a science-y person; I hated chemistry and I never went near physics—I didn't think I could handle it, and it wasn't pertinent at the time. But it is now, and it's worth paying attention to physics, because it's opened up a whole new avenue of work. The Peruvians tapped into it for their weaving, with all those beautiful gauzes, but it hasn't happened before in the knitting world. I spend a lot of time thinking about the physical part of the work. A lot of people go right by that; they don't even think about their yarn—they think about the color and the size, but they don't think about the physicalness of it and how it can affect their work. Even wrapping and looping yarn around your needle changes your surface. I think it's because I'm a spinner that I really consider the qualities of yarn. Before I started to spin, I didn't even consider if my yarn was plied or single-strand.

This is a little top; it's cashmere. See how it looks like it's herringbone? It's S's and Z's. Some are spun clockwise, and some are spun counterclockwise. I did four rows of this one and four rows of this one—as long as you keep your rows and number of stitches equal, geometrically and numerically, it stays on grain and you'll get a straight piece of cloth. I knew that I could get these interesting surfaces with the energy I put in my yarns when I made them; then it was just a matter of sampling with types of fibers and using different knit/purl patterns. It's explorative, and it's *exciting*. [A trunk is propped open on its side in a corner of Kathryn's studio. From a rack inside it hang several of her creations. She takes one out—an all-white sweater, the monochrome look of which is a stark contrast to the myriad colors of her other knitted garments.]

This is stockinette stitch that looks nothing like stockinette. This is a four-inch rib that looks nothing like a four-inch rib. This is the entrelac peak that I came up with; and this is the same thing with a different directional—with one you get a peak, with the other you get a swirl. You can change a surface that's been traditional for so long, with no new skill. There is a little bit of physics you have to be aware of, because when you wrap yarn around the needle, you either take energy out of it or put it in; you have to pay attention. But it's really simple, and it gives you knowledge that you can use to take your knitting to another level.

I don't make things to sell them—I couldn't care less if they sell, because if they don't, they'll be in my private collection. I just make things that I love to make and that'll look good on me. In the meantime, I have all these cool clothes to wear.

Ready, Set, Lace

Better than a hundred years lived in idleness and in weakness is a single day of life lived with . . . powerful striving.

—THE DHAMMAPADA

And yet, somehow, I still couldn't muster the enthusiasm (or stamina, or patience) to tackle a "real" project. So I gave myself another swatching challenge: Star Rib Mesh. The pattern was not complicated in and of itself—just repeating rows of slip stitches and yarn-overs—but to create the maximum lacy effect, I chose to use the tiny, fussy, blue kid mohair from Edith's shop and a pair of #10 plastic needles that Elanor had given me.

I wasn't merely interested in trying my hand at a difficult pattern. I had also come to realize that over and over, the knitting I'd seen that had dazzled me the most, had made me catch my breath in astonishment, had been fashioned of intricate lace patterns: Susan Haviland's painstaking, columnar shawl; another shawl, a gunmetal gray beauty by Elanor in a diagonal Falling Vine stitch; a series of enormous, willowy, cobwebby wall hangings I'd come across in a book one day while I was doing research at the Metropolitan Museum's Costume Institute library. What is it about lace that entrances me so? The lightness, the detail, the almost calligraphic motion of the yarn as it flows and loops, leading the eye gracefully up and over and down and up. The look of lace—the vertiginousness of lace—makes my heart skip a beat.

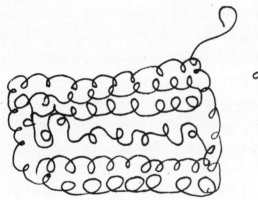

I'm sure I had an inkling before I even began the Mesh pattern that I was setting myself up for absolute aggravation. And that's exactly what I got. The fine fuzz of the mohair caught on itself as I knit, allowing the stitches no breath, no elasticity; and the yarn also stuck, like Velcro, to the plastic needles. With almost every stitch I had to stop, tease the next loop open with my fingernail in order to insert the needle, and check and recheck which strand of the fine yarn was the one I needed to catch to make a stitch. Over and over I lost count. I discovered that I couldn't tell back from front, knit from purl, because the fine yarn made every stitch practically transparent and, for all practical purposes, identical. Finally, I was so lost I couldn't go on. After two hours and only a few rows, I had to pull everything out. But no matter how gingerly I pulled, or how I tried to coax the stitches loose, I could not get the knitting—intractable as knots in thread—to unravel. I was finally forced to admit defeat and to break the whole mess off the ball.

I didn't get much further on the next go-round, even after I switched to #11 aluminum needles, which at least had the benefit of not clinging to the yarn. I wound up with another tangle, which I broke off again, and then a third. I decided to try the same pattern with the red and yellow Altamira from Artfibers. This time, I experienced the added hassle of the double ply, and figuring out where to place my needle became an agonizing chore. No surprise: That swatch met the same fate as the earlier blue ones.

Why, why did I go on? Because I was so thoroughly annoyed by now that there was no way I was going to give up, give in. I'd spent hours at this task already; I couldn't face the prospect of having nothing to show for it. I went back to the kid mohair and cast on with the #11 needles. I put my needles down, took a drink of water, closed my eyes, and tried to relax. Then I began to knit, ever so slowly; and slowly, rows of Mesh began to emerge. I began to feel relief at last. Sometime later, having reminded myself to breathe and relax with almost every passing moment, I managed to complete a small, C-shaped swatch of Mesh. It looks handsome to me now, months later, when I'm no longer held in the grip of frustration, as I swivel it around my wrist and contemplate its curlicue meanderings. And I marvel that something so tiny once commanded the better part of a day, and that something so apparently innocuous—just a few loopy rows of pale color—could have inspired in me such extreme annoyance.

10.

Records of a Knitting Family

I happened to mention to Twisted Sister Barbara Levin that I'd been hoping to interview kids who knit, and two days later she sent me a post from an online discussion group: "My daughter Lizzy is twelve years old. She learned how to knit five years ago from her grandma. Lizzy has chosen a special project to do in celebration of her Bat Mitzvah . . . collecting scarves and hats to send to the soldiers in Afghanistan. . . . [She] hopes to have at least 200+." I contacted Lizzy's mom, Cathy, and discovered that she knit, too, and that her own mother—the very same grandma who had taught Lizzy to knit—was visiting them from Missouri. What a stroke of luck—a whole knitting family, all in one place.

Contemplating the letters that this generational triumvirate sent to me in response to a lengthy questionnaire, I found myself nostalgic for something that had never been: my mother, my grandmother, and me, knitting away in my grandmother's lair-like New Hampshire living room, offering advice, encouragement, and applause, but mostly just basking in one another's company.

CATHY BROWNSTEIN

[W]hen we can practice even one art, with accuracy, and comfort to ourselves . . . we have gained a resource which very few women will not find a thousand occasions of appreciating.

—MRS. PULLMAN, *THE LADY'S MANUAL OF FANCY WORK*, 1859

I was seven years old when I learned to knit; my mother taught me. My mother is the best knitter I know. She is fast and knows a lot about the whole knitting/crocheting art. She is very, very dedicated to this love, and it shows. I am also so pleased that she got both of my daughters interested in it. My older daughter is too busy to knit right now, but she knows how. My younger daughter, Lizzy, loves it just like my mother.

My mother has always knitted and made beautiful things. When my children were young—one year, three years, five years of age—she would send them things for making needlepoint: yarn, needles, all sorts of things. Then she started sending yarn—boxes and boxes of it. My kids loved it. They would use this beautiful yarn to make cobwebs all over their rooms. They would tie yarn *everywhere*. It was adorable; they had the best time having this beautiful yarn to play with. Lizzy, when she turned three or four, started knitting with her fingers—something my mother taught her.

I knit with my daughter, my mother, my sister. I love this time together. It is a very special thing to have my daughter enjoy something just like my mother and I do. I stopped knitting for several years and just started again in the last few months because of Lizzy's scarf project for the soldiers in Afghanistan. After making eight of them in a month and a half, I would like to make something else, but right now scarves are all Lizzy and I will make for the next four or five months.

I don't spend the time like my mother does to be an awesome knitter. I love picking out the yarn and finishing the project; I am not so interested in all the work. Even though I do enjoy the process at times, the end result is much more rewarding to me. I am faster and better today than three months ago, just because I do it so much. One day, I would like to knit or crochet baby clothes for my grandchildren—when I have them.

LIZZY BROWNSTEIN

Knitting articles for soldier boys and fathers and mothers makes a person feel very much account.

—JANE EAGRE FRYER, *THE MARY FRANCES BOOK OF KNITTING AND CROCHET OR ADVENTURES AMONG THE KNITTING PEOPLE*, 1918

I learned to knit when I was seven years old. My grandmother taught me. I loved it but thought it was challenging. I love to challenge myself, so I stuck with it and it became easier. I never knew there was such a thing called knitting before I learned.

I knit with my mother and my grandmother, whenever she is in town. I like it because we sometimes just sit, knit, laugh, talk, or watch TV with one another, and I have two helpers if I mess up, so that always helps.

I first made a scarf for my dad. It was funny to see the way it turned out, and now I compare it to recent projects. That first scarf was not always even; it had extra stitches sometimes, or sometimes it didn't have enough stitches. It was also exciting to think, *I made that!* I do eventually want to knit better and faster, but that takes time, passion, and devotion. I define "getting better" as not having holes in anything and having scarves be all the same width the whole way.

Next year I am turning thirteen, and for a Jewish child, this is a big step. You have your Bar/Bat Mitzvah and you need to do a good deed. I chose to knit scarves and send them to soldiers in mountain training camps in Afghanistan. My mom and I were thinking about something fun that would also help someone else, and my mom started listing my hobbies. Then she asked, "Why don't you make scarves and send them to soldiers?" I thought it was a great idea, so I got onto an army website and e-mailed them. When I didn't get a response, it just so happened that my dad was going to Fort Lauderdale for business; he talked to someone who told him that he could get me an address to mail the scarves to. The address was for a mountain training camp. So I had my project all planned out and ready to go. Between my mom and me, we have knit about twenty to twenty-five scarves; we are planning to knit a lot, maybe even a couple hundred. I need all the scarves to be done by November 1 so I can send them to the soldiers in time for when it gets cold. I am having lots of other people help, too. I have posted about my project on two websites, and I have many relatives who have said they would make a couple scarves.

The one main reason I knit is to have fun. Knitting has always calmed me down when I was stressed. I don't care what type of mood I am in, if I have spare time, I love to knit. If I'm knitting scarves for someone else, it always reminds me how fortunate I am to be able to help that person. For me, the joy of knitting begins when I plan a project. For example, I'm knitting scarves for soldiers in Afghanistan, and I was excited just thinking about the project that lies on the path ahead of me. That is when it first begins, but there is always joy throughout the process: picking out yarn, casting on, knitting, binding off, stitching it, and sending the scarves away. There is always joy.

I have always wanted a pair of my own socks. From the beginning, though, I have always knit for others, so I never get around to it. After I make myself a pair, I might wear them whenever I knit.

[T]he real purpose [of knitting is to] provid[e] comforts for the men who are going forth to fight, and the happiness it gives to hundreds of women who are gladly availing themselves of this opportunity to "do their bit" and offer real service. . . .

THE MODERN PRISCILLA MAGAZINE, 1917

SALLY SINGER

Most people have an obsession. Mine is knitting.

—ELIZABETH ZIMMERMANN, *KNITTING*

WITHOUT TEARS, 1971 (1995)

I love the fact that my granddaughter, Lizzy, is so thrilled with her knitting and that her mom is helping her complete her projects. Actually, Lizzy is a better knitter than her mom and loves it more. I also have a granddaughter in college who's aiming toward being a medical doctor. She loves knitting to help her relax after tremendous work and to amaze her friends with her talents. She's great, too.

I first learned to knit when I was eight years old and was taught by my grandmother. I loved it straight off. I used to pretend to be sick (I even ate soap for effect) so I could stay home from school and knit. I never did think it was complicated—just fun, relaxing, and so very creative. When I was older and the Second World War started, I began to knit socks and blankets for our servicemen. I felt as though I was helping, and, being a young girl, I imagined a handsome young soldier wearing my hand-knit socks. It was so romantic. In my teens, I began to knit argyle socks for my boyfriends, but most didn't hang around long enough for me to finish a pair.

When I was fifteen years old, I made a whole twenty-piece layette for my hope chest. I have never stopped knitting and always have ten to twenty projects going at one time, so no matter what I want to knit, be it scarf, shawl, slippers, socks, mittens, hats, sweaters, throws, children's sweaters (I have eighteen grandchildren), or toys, I have something to work on. Anything that can be knitted, I will try. I now have a beautiful Knitaly sweater to start from a pattern in *Knitting Now*. I also have four pairs of socks that are half done, a Hanne Falkenburg jacket half through, and four other sweaters and two throws. I cannot go a day without knitting. I am a knitter. That describes me completely.

You will never know it all as a knitter. I take classes from Meg Swanson, Lily Chin, Joan Schrouder, and many others. I am always trying to improve and change and create with my knitting. Otherwise, it is just hobby, but the way I do it, it's a real passion. I will never stop learning and will never, never tire of it. I wake up in the morning anxious to knit. I knit while I walk and I knit while I am visiting and I knit when I go to parties, restaurants, doctor appointments, play games, and anything else that gives me enough time to knit a row or two or more. I learn something from every project no matter how small it is. I might learn that I really don't enjoy a certain yarn that I have wanted to use for a long time; I might learn that I am more creative than I thought; I might learn that life is beautiful no matter what, when I can create and touch yarn.

Knitting is very calming and very soothing, and no pill can do that for me. It is a real comfort to me, and I look forward to the time I can sit down with music, a movie, or a good book and knit away. I can knit without looking, if the project isn't too complicated. I knit when I am sad, happy, worried—it helps me. But when my husband died six years ago, I didn't knit for six months. He loved my knitting so much, and I even taught him to knit. I just couldn't face anything without him. But I am better now, and I know that he would be so happy to have me "knit just one more row"—I always said that to him when he wanted to go somewhere.

I think about a project as I am driving through the spring fields in Missouri; I plan a sweater among the beautiful spring colors. I don't live near a yarn shop, and so I have to drive 200 miles each way to visit one, but it is worth it. I will spend four to six hours touching, feeling, looking, and talking to all the customers. Then I finally make a purchase, never much under $500, and plan which project I shall cast on first. First I pick up one of my 125 knitting bags, and then wind the yarn and gather the needles, markers, and any other accessory I may need, and then I cast on and love every single stitch I make. Putting garments together used to be a job, a job that I didn't look forward to. Now I work on multiple items, and when I complete five of them (I keep them all in one big knitting bag), I spend a whole day assembling and blocking, and it is really a lot of fun, and I feel so good to have five completed objects. It takes the sting out of finishing, and I look forward to the whole process.

I love to follow patterns—to some degree. I very seldom use the yarn called for, and I like to change small things: color, design, length, or fit. So in a way I am designing, but there are so many wonderful designers out there, and they are all so productive that I love to use their patterns. I admire anyone who plans the whole thing, but I love the knitting and selecting of the yarn so much that I really don't want to spend time with figures.

Beautiful colors in nature inspire me: trees, water, clouds, snow. Almost everywhere I go, I see something I think would make a wonderful sweater. Inspiration is all around us, and I admire people like Kaffe Fassett, who can see beauty everywhere.

I really do knit all the time. I even carry it from room to room to complete a row or when I just don't want to put it down. I also take it to the dentist's office with me. I hate going to the dentist, so I hold my knitting and really enjoy the feel of the yarn as he is drilling. It distracts me and I can knit a hat during a cleaning and filling. That helps me and keeps me calm.

I am not a project knitter. The process of knitting is the fun, and the finished project is just the frosting on the cake. I always finish a project eventually. I just finished a Christmas stocking that I started in 1989, and it is beautiful. I have hundreds of skeins of yarn and more than a hundred kits that are all just waiting to be knit up into something beautiful, but I find the yarn by itself is also beautiful. I sold my dining set and filled the dining room with baskets and shelves of yarn, and I have a

19' x 35' second-floor studio, and it is filled. Every room has projects in baskets. Each phone has a bag by it with socks so I can do mindless knitting while on the phone.

And, of course, I love to talk about my knitting. This is a subject I know and love.

Learning to Love Mistakes

Where there is creation there is progress. Where there is no creation there is no progress: know the nature of creation.

Where there is joy there is creation. Where there is no joy there is no creation: know the nature of joy.

—THE UPANISHADS

I banished the snippet of Star Rib Mesh from my sight. And, as it had been a giant headache (and finger ache) to carry off, I had no desire to jump right back in with more of the same: with an openwork Diamond Mesh, say, or a delicate scalloped wonder, like Shower Stitch, whose instructions read, not at all optimistically, "There is a 'p3 tog-b' in Rows 4 and 8 which might prove a little awkward. . . ." Awkward—not at all a condition I was looking to tackle when I was still nursing wounds from the unruly mohair thread.

However, there was one pattern I'd been longing to make since the very first time I'd opened the Barbara Walker book. I hadn't yet been ready—I'd first needed to get a firm grasp on such vocabulary as "ssk" and "p2sso" and to understand that directions in parentheses were to be repeated, and to realize that mistakes in the instructions come up now and then, and that if I trusted my growing ability in pattern reading, I

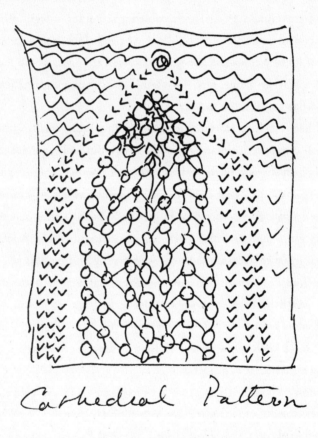

Cathedral Pattern

could recognize them and fix them. In short, I needed confidence and experience, and also to discover for myself, and to really understand, that there is nothing impossible in knitting (with the possible exception of achieving satisfaction with fine-gauge mohair); no matter what other elements you add, you will always be simply knitting and purling.

The pattern that had caught my eye all those months ago, and which I turned to gawp at every time I opened the book, was Cathedral Pattern. It was a graceful, lace-filled arch, cabled up its sides, woven into a garter-stitch background, with a bobble at its peak. Not frail and wispy like some of its lacy cousins, Cathedral Pattern, I thought, would look best if I used a thicker-gauge yarn—something easygoing and malleable, precisely what I was in the mood for.

When I'd first started knitting, cabling—like making lace—had seemed to me the ultimate in complication. But as I'd gone (sometimes) merrily knitting and purling along, it dawned on me that one anticipated problem—the fact that I didn't own a cabling needle—wasn't really a problem at all. Surely a regular knitting needle, or a thin pencil, or even a safety pin, would provide a perfectly adequate substitute. Another problem was my own aversion to unnecessary complication. But as I explored the workings of certain patterns, I realized that a cable pattern, like any other, could be broken down into its most basic elements—knit and purl. Even a bobble was made by taking a small bit of fabric and knitting it back and forth a few times. Making a cable, I convinced myself, was merely a matter of concentrating.

I don't know if it was some act of release from the thin mohair, or the fact of my long-standing desire to knit this pattern, or some fortuitous alignment of the planets, but Cathedral Pattern was the most fun, most liberating piece of knitting I'd so far completed. I made it through all forty-two rows without stopping, without pulling out, without annoyance. The cabling—some eight brief rows in all that incorporated both front and back crosses—was, as I'd convinced myself it would be, a simple matter of paying attention: slipping a couple stitches onto a third needle, then knitting or purling them back in. And the same held true for the bobble.

The finished rectangle was some six inches tall and four inches wide. I was so delighted with it that I carried it around with me for hours after I'd cast off, taking it into the kitchen to admire it when it was time to cook dinner; over to the phone, to poke my fingers through its lace center as I talked with friends; fiddling with the bobble later that night as I sat in front of the TV. Later, close inspection revealed that I'd made two mistakes: At the bottom of one of the arch's pillars, I had twisted a couple stitches, creating a gash across the otherwise smooth knitting, and about halfway up the arch, I'd dropped one stitch. The mistakes hardly bothered me. What's more, it occurred to me that as with anything I make—paintings or birthday cards or decorated cakes—my mistakes are my fingerprint. They are how I am able to recognize my work as my own, and they offer, ultimately, a perverse kind of comfort.

11.

More Summer Days:
New York

"I'm hot for the yarn," Callie Janoff explained to me, pulling a mass of lusciously colored Prussian blue stuff—an antique find, filled with moth holes—out of a plastic shopping bag. We were sitting on a park bench in Williamsburg, Brooklyn, on an absurdly humid and windy afternoon, shvitzing ever so slightly and yelling over the wind and the noise of a gaggle of ball-tossing day-campers about what kind of work, exactly, was involved in making a sweater from such a hopeless wreck of a yarn stash (a lot of splicing together—no surprise there). Callie seemed nonplussed by the challenge.

"I really strive to make my life a creative act, to not break it up so much: Now I'm doing art, now I'm not," said Callie, a graduate of the Art Institute of Chicago, as she fondled the yarn—nothing special to look at at first glance, but on deeper contemplation, pleasingly mellowed with age to a gray-tinged hue. Callie is also one of the founders of the Church of Craft, the very same organization that spawned Allison Dalton's congregation back in Los Angeles. On the organization's website (motto:

"... from apse to zipper"), there's a sermon by Callie posted, which goes a long way toward summing up her feelings about knitting and crafting and life generally: "We come together, and we make things, and we affirm the craft we see in each other. Then we go home inspired . . . and we live our lives with all the happiness and love we can."

CALLIE JANOFF

Perhaps the hectic pace of modern life leads people to seek moments of peaceful satisfaction in the ancient disciplines of making.
—BARBARA WALKER, *A SECOND TREASURY OF KNITTING PATTERNS*, 1970 (1998)

I've always been a giver-awayer. Growing up, it was always a way to connect with somebody, and as a little kid I gave away a lot of presents to people I cared about. Gifts were always really important in our lives; it was a big way my family expressed how they felt about one another. I've always considered that the things I did, the drawings I made, were best used when they belonged to someone else. A lot of what I made I would make with a particular person in mind, and then it would become a gift for that person. As for knitting, I had no use for five scarves and two pairs of mittens, but I wanted them to exist in the world, so I made them for other people.

Is the gift you make that takes you ten minutes less valuable than the gift that took you 100 hours? To me, it doesn't matter how long it takes, it's more about the idea and the sentiment and the intention. That seems right, and when somebody gives me a gift, it's so precious to me to know that they spent this time thinking about me. I think that's all a gift is for, to let somebody know that you care about them. There's nothing sadder than wasting craft, and I try really hard not to give people things they don't want. I don't make things for people without asking them what color they want or asking them if this is something they would wear.

Several people tried to teach me to knit throughout my life, without much success. I've watched women try to teach their daughters how to knit—it's really hard to show somebody you're that close to and that intimate with how to do something and to give them enough space to learn the way that they need to. I think that's why maybe it never stuck for me. If it had been presented in a different way, like, "Here's this tool, and these are the different skills you need to create this thing," I might have been interested. But also, knitting wasn't a big part of growing up in the '70s in California. California wasn't a big, wooly kind of place; it was more of a macramé kind of place. A scarf is your first knitting project. I never needed a scarf.

I've been crocheting all along. I learned how to crochet when I was a little kid and was always comfortable with yarn and hooks. Crochet is about making loops, and it's bunchier—it's almost like making a sculpture. Knitting is more like making a painting. They're apples and oranges to me. Some things need to be crocheted; some things need to be knitted. They have really different qualities. I think knitted sweaters are more comfortable, because they have elasticity and they move with your body, whereas crochet is better for things that you want to be really stable: a frog closure, for example.

I started knitting about three years ago, after I moved to New York. I just freaked out that I was sitting there making fabric, and I could take it on the subway. It was kind of empowering, too: "Here's another thing I can do." It was so collective consciousness. Everyone I knew had started knitting. I taught myself one night; I found that was the best way for me to learn. I bought myself a book—a stapled little 8½" x 11" book called *Learn to Knit* that cost $4 at the yarn store. I was able to follow the pictures, and I taught myself American style. It was really easy for me to pick up once I'd seen the pictures. I think I needed to sort of muddle through it without everybody saying no this, yes that, no this, yes that. I needed to make my own mistakes and go at my own pace. Once I could do it, then I could have people show me the tricky stuff, like how to do yarn-overs or how to do different styles of cast-on.

The first thing I knit was a scarf. I made my friend a scarf and it was purple and it had tassels, and then I wanted to put her name at the bottom of it. I wasn't following a pattern; I was like, "I want it to be this wide," and I had read the part in the book on gauge, so I just did it. It took me a while to get into the pattern idea, but not too long. The first pattern I followed was a mitten pattern—I jumped right into mittens, I don't know what I was thinking. I had done some circular hats and I just kind of winged that; I didn't know what I was doing. But I was able to translate a lot of what I understood about crochet and put it into knitting right away.

Last summer, I started making a sweater. It was multicolored with a lot of action—red, yellow, navy, orange, with a few other random colors thrown in—a little cap sleeve number made of squares and triangles and hexagons. It was a happy sweater. Someone I worked with died just a week into it. About a month later, my grandfather died. At some point in the first couple months of making this sweater, I looked down at it in the subway and realized every stitch I had made was like a little tiny moment of grief and suffering in my life, and that I had made this thing out of these moments of grief and suffering. Once the sweater was done, it wasn't sad anymore, and wearing it doesn't make me sad; it makes me really happy. I can look at all those moments and remember what I was thinking and know that I don't have to feel that way anymore. That was a really important thing to realize, that I had unconsciously translated an experience into this thing I was doing with my hands. And I felt better.

Every moment has its own intensity, and every stitch is like every moment to me. When you make something, it's infused with whatever is happening around you at that time. When you make something, it has everything to do with everything. I'm a real believer in the connectedness of life and energy, and I think there's an impact, a correlation between a choice you make or a way that you handle something and what you're thinking about and feeling. Making things makes me feel better because it's satisfying, because I can look at this thing I've done and know that it's all about me, that every moment I experienced is somehow infused in there. I've accomplished something. You can break the accomplishment up however you want: I knit this much; that's an accomplishment. I knit this and put it together; that's an accomplishment. I tried this and it didn't work so I ripped it out; that's an accomplishment, too. You can find a sense of accomplishment anywhere you need to.

My friend Tristy and I cofounded the Church of Craft a couple years ago. We're a community of people who organize ourselves around our love of making things, any things. We focus on enjoying and appreciating the creativity that happens in our everyday lives. The idea came to me when some friends of mine wanted to get married and they couldn't find somebody to perform the ceremony who they felt good about, who they felt understood the kind of people they were and were able to incorporate the level of spirituality they wanted. So we talked about it, and they decided to ask me if I would get ordained and perform the ceremony, which of course, I was delighted to do—*beside* myself to do. So I went ahead and got ordained, and I think I went into it thinking of its performance value. At the time, I was interested in doing artwork that had a performative quality, that was about the space between things, and interactions between people, and trying to blur the line between art and life, so this seemed really perfect for me. Then I got down to doing it and it was not like any art I had done before. There was no artistic distance or abstraction, there was no process through which this was filtered. It was very real. Very intense. And really moving. It was a totally life-changing experience.

It made me sad that these people who were close friends of mine didn't have a place that served their needs—there was no minister or pastor or rabbi or clergy-person they could go to to have this really important thing accomplished. That seemed unfair; just because my friends and I don't identify with organized religion doesn't mean we're not spiritual people. So out of that grew the desire to provide that service, not just for weddings but for people in their spiritual lives. That, for me, is what the Church of Craft is for—to serve those people for whom creativity is an aspect of spirituality. My belief is more that God, or the

Spirit, lives within us and is part of everything, like The Force from *Star Wars*. My way of connecting with that energy and that power is to be very in touch with myself, to know myself well. I feel the most in touch with my own inner person when I'm making things and being creative.

From day one, from the first time the Church of Craft met, people were bananas for this idea. People who are into it are incredibly into it—it really struck a chord. We started with our friends, and they told their friends, and word got out, and people started showing up. Now I don't know most of the people who come. They just found us. A typical meeting is pretty low-key: We get together and we make stuff. Inevitably, conversations pick up about what it is we're doing and why we're there. There's not anything so special about our meetings except the intention. We're getting together because it's fun. People can enter into it in any way they want to. For me, the idea is to make it really easy for people to find that sense of accomplishment, that sense of "I made this," which is so powerful for people who spend their entire lives doing a tiny piece of cog-in-the-wheel work. This is a chance to share with people that joy of making.

There are a lot of yarn crafters who come and knit or crochet, and I think that is partly a function of how portable and easy these things are to do, and there's a lot of support for them. Some of the people are artists, some of them are not: They work at all kinds of jobs all over the city, and they have different lives and different agendas, and it's fantastic to see all of them hanging out with one another in the same place. They're genuinely happy and interested in what other people are doing. It is all about community, and that's so valuable. I never realized it before. I always valued my friendships and my circle of friends, but I never thought of them as a *community*. Being involved in this project, and being a knitter as well, and knowing that there is a tremendous community of knitters is really powerful. It's important; it makes me feel connected.

 Mincing no words, Kirsten sat right down in the chair opposite me at a table in an Alphabet City, New York, coffee shop and started to talk knitting, which she'd recently been forced to give up (temporarily) due to a repetitive stress injury. She's an editor at getcrafty. com, a how-to website that proposes to "make art out of everyday life," and which will instruct you how to knit a summer shawl, a bikini, or an '80s sweater, how to "bake like a Zen Buddhist" and "thrift like an expert." Kirsten's also a member of the Church of Craft, and the New York Stitch 'n' Bitch group. And—as if that weren't enough—she's a student of feng shui. In addition to all that, I found her to be a typical native New Yorker, a rare breed and one that I also happen to belong to—opinionated and blunt, qualities I cherish. My favorite of her admissions about knitting: "I'm crap at this." And as is the way in the best of interviews, I found that I barely had to mention a topic for her to tackle it and wrestle it to the ground.

KIRSTEN HUDSON

*This elegant art cannot fail to
hold a high place among what
may be termed the* Manual
Accomplishments *of ladies,
from the beauty, variety, and durability
of the articles fabricated, not less than
from the extreme facility of execution.*
—MRS. PULLMAN, *THE LADY'S
MANUAL OF FANCY WORK, 1859*

I learned to crochet because I didn't think I could learn to knit. I
thought, *Crochet is easier.* I knew from my mother that you can just
pull it out. I felt knitting was beyond me. I tried to learn how to knit on
a disastrous . . . well, the trip wasn't disastrous, but learning to knit was. I
went to Turkey with a friend of mine, and we decided it would be a great
way to meet women, to talk to women we wouldn't ordinarily meet. We
thought it would be safe to approach other women if they were knitting,
and that was totally true. My friend knew how to knit, so I bought a
bunch of stuff, and she tried to teach me. She came home with a sweater.
I came home with this mangled bit of dirty, really vile stuff. I couldn't
get it; I couldn't get it at all. I thought, *It's beyond me; I'm crap at this; I
can't do it.* And I didn't like it; I didn't feel as though I needed to do it.

Then I got really inspired to learn how to knit because this woman
Johanna, another Church of Craft person, does this amazing thing she

calls "method knitting," in which she uses all these different yarns and huge needles, and it goes really, really fast, and you can make these beautiful scarves and hats. That appealed to me, the aesthetic and the different yarns and the speed. I really wanted to learn that. I tried to learn to knit again and failed again. Then Callie suggested that I learn continental; I don't know why she suggested that, but it worked. I haven't mastered purling yet. I do know how to purl, but I hate it so much that I stopped. It feels awkward; it doesn't flow; it doesn't make sense to me the way knitting does. Continental knitting is just about making this one movement, and purling seems to have this other step in there that I can't get my head around. And since I don't know how to knit well enough to fix problems or to even see them, it just makes a mess as soon as I start purling. I'm going to give that a go again really soon, though, because now I'm a little embarrassed about the fact that I can't purl.

I had some ideas in my head about things that I wanted to make. Also, I was really keen on the idea of having something to do on the train—I really liked the idea that knitting was something to do while I did something else, and I had seen all these beautiful things that people had made. Most of the crafting I do is more general crafting: cutting things up and putting them back together, or the kind of crafting that's about telling somebody else what you want and saying, "Now you do it," which is my favorite kind. I'm also, in general in my life, trying to be more about process, and it seemed to be a nice dovetailing, to be able to make something that wouldn't exist otherwise and to be involved in the process—not just buying it or having someone else do it. It's nice to have some sort of control of my freedom of expression and to trust in myself a little bit more, because I don't have a lot of trust. I tend to think of myself as a failed intellectual, somebody who's all ideas and no stuff, no thing, no product.

Crocheting was safe because I could pull it out. I stuck with it, because a lot of the way I learned was: You can't go wrong; it just doesn't matter with crochet. You can put the needle anywhere; it's incredibly open-ended. It's similar with the method knitting, in that mistakes don't show up as much and it plays to my strengths. Aesthetically, I would say color and texture—I'm really good at that. And I love having things that I've made, and I really love being able to give people things that I've made. I've learned through knitting how to be better about pulling things out and starting again. This is why I always want other people to do it, because I figure they know how to do it already. They know how to make this, so they won't have this issue of making it wrong. In theory. Whereas it will take me several tries and a longer time to get it right, so why bother?

This goes back to my mother, who always put the fear of knitting into me by saying, "In knitting, if you make a mistake, you have to knit backwards." I just felt that I never wanted to knit backward. People often tell me that things are easy, which I get excited about, but crafting does not come easily; it's really hard for me. I have a deep mistrust when people tell me things are easy when it involves making things. Which is also what knitting's about—getting over these fears and being someone who makes things.

There's certainly a political aspect—not wanting to be so much of a consumer, wanting to be engaged. There's also another aspect, which is that I have a lot of images in my head, and for much of my life, if I haven't been able to find someone to realize them for me, they just sort of ate away at me and I felt very powerless, unable to do anything about them. I'm gradually kind of crawling my way into knowledge about how to make things. In part, it's about not being so powerless anymore, and in part it's about acknowledging myself as someone who is creative and who is not just about ideas. Partially, it's also feedback: I make it; I get satisfied about it; and so now that I've had that satisfaction, I do it again. My first method scarf was such an amazing thing—I was like, "*Gaaah*... I love it!"—that I wanted to do it again.

I've always been really good at a lot of things, and whenever I come across something that I'm not good at right away, my impulse is to leave it. I chalk it up to "I can't do it." It's in the realm of Why bother? I'm good at all these other things; why would I waste time attempting to do this? The appearance of failure—I hate that. The whole "Never let 'em see you sweat" thing; I'm trying to change that. If the things I'm good at had been satisfying, then I might not have come to a place where I was willing to try other things. The things I am good at, a lot of them I hate doing: writing, being an academic—I dropped out of a Ph.D. program. I'm very good at school, and I'm good at being organized. I came up against enough walls where I realized, "I hate this; I don't know why I'm doing this." Sometimes I'll write as a favor to someone, and I'll hate it, but I'll be glad I did it. But I can't do that for my life. That's not a life, that's a project.

I was becoming deeply unsatisfied. I always felt that I was not physically good at making things, and I abandoned it. Then I decided to take it up in a serious way and to learn how to do things and be willing to do them badly. A lot of my approach to it is, "I'm crap at this, and if it comes out well, all the better." I'm fairly overtly up-front about the fact that knitting is not my forte. But now I'm starting to get comfortable. I've learned to knit in public, and it's difficult to have that on display. Most of the learning—book learning—I've done in private. I don't particularly look like a knitter, but I think I would be uncomfortable if I were dressed conservatively and I was knitting—then it would be like I was pretending to be someone I wasn't. That would make me uncomfortable.

The knitting itself I like; it helps me focus. It helps keep my mind from wandering. That's been a really nice discovery, to find that I can occupy my hands and then my mind calms down. If I don't have a book or I don't want to read—a lot of my need to knit comes from my own inability to just do nothing. I don't think knitting is meditative, but it is calming; it makes me present, makes me more available to hear things. Maybe it helps me focus on something outside myself. I find that I can't talk and knit, but I can listen.

What I can't get my head around are people who knit a plain white sweater. The excitement to me is that this is something that didn't exist before, and it's coming into being, and I don't know exactly what it's going to be. But with a white sweater, I know *exactly* what it's going to be. When I'm making a hat, there's an interesting point at the top and an interesting point at the bottom; sometimes I'll lose interest in the middle and think, *Have I made it long enough? Have I done enough yet to make the other part?* The method knitting maintains my interest throughout the whole thing. I think I might go back to learning afghan squares—something I never thought I had the patience for—because I'm interested in how they come into being. My problem is counting: I always lose track. Sometimes I'm conflicted about it—I'm not sure I want to focus so much on just that. I want to be a little bit looser. But I'm kind of interested in that kind of magic, seeing those squares turn into something else.

There's a part of me that thinks that there doesn't need to be a distinction between "Someone gave me this" and "Someone made me this." But when you give somebody something you've made, it has a better chance of having a powerful meaning. Occasionally I've made things for people, but it's more like I make a bazillion hats and a bazillion scarves, and if somebody says, "I really like that," I just give it to them. That feels like it's a pure giving. If I'm all about the process, they can just have it. I think it's sort of like that practice in certain cultures in which if you admire something in somebody's home, they just give it to you—that's what it's there for. I create it, and it's there to find its home. There are things I enjoy making so much that I make them to give to everyone. I have this yarn I really like, and a scarf is pretty easy to make, and people just love it—they go nutty for it. It's really safe, because everybody likes it and I like making it. I try to be clear with all the gifts I give that I've made that I'm not bothered if someone gives it away, because I don't want it languishing. I don't want it to become clutter. I want to put it in circulation.

 It was Lana Le, another Church of Crafter who knows both Kirsten and Callie, who told me about Rita Bobry. A little more than a year ago, Rita opened Downtown Yarns on Avenue A in Manhattan's East Village, across the street from the coffee shop where Stitch 'n' Bitch NY holds its meetings. It's the same coffee shop in which I'd been interviewing

Kirsten, and after we were through talking, I decided to stop in to introduce myself.

I almost walked by the shop—would have walked by it if I hadn't been very specifically looking for it. It's a tiny storefront painted green at its trim, showing to the street only a screen door on the left and a modestly sized vitrine on the right—filled, I realized, once I'd managed to spot the place, with little hats shaped like pumpkins and raspberries. The afternoon of my drop-in, I found Rita having a serious conversation with a chic Japanese woman—a devoted customer and also a clothing designer—who was about to take off on a month-long trip to Tokyo and wanted to make sure that Rita would hold on to the armful of yarn she'd selected until her return.

So small in appearance from the street, inside the shop looked just right—oddly spacious, cheerfully lit, stacked to the ceiling with wool and cashmere and cotton. There was no one else around but Rita's sweet-faced golden retriever, Frankie, and the room seemed to breathe with calm.

I returned a week later, on a humid evening, to considerable chaos. Customers streamed in and out, the shop's "Knitting Doctor" stood by, waiting for that night's project class to arrive—and they did, quickly filling up the back table and loudly, chipperly taking over the whole latter half of the shop—and Frankie, eager for her evening walk, paced the floor and whimpered at the street. I sat at the rear counter with Lana, a graphic designer who works at the shop one day a week, and Rita, who was distracted by the constant onslaught of questions and purchases and requests for class schedules. No longer a peaceful oasis, the shop had become feverishly alive, a vibrant and impossible-to-miss extension of the neighborhood.

Downtown Yarns

Let me warn you that a genuine interest in knitting can keep you fasci-
nated, eagerly pursuing it and never satisfied through a lifetime. If a
woman knew all there was to know about knitting there would be little un-
der the sun she didn't know.

—ROSE WILDER LANE, *WOMAN'S DAY BOOK OF*

AMERICAN NEEDLEWORK, 1963

RITA BOBRY: I've always knit, always done things with my hands throughout my life. My grandma taught me, so I knit for as long as can remember—not steadily but on and off. The last cycle of knitting, I don't remember where I got my yarn, but before that I would go to Grand Street on the other side of Houston Street [in New York City], and there were a million knitting stores there. There was Sunray, there was Bell Yarn, there was another one. One was quite large; people would come from all over the city for it. One was more neighborhoody, with these older ladies working there. In the way of those days, they would teach people to knit by writing a paragraph pattern, and they'd say, "Do that and come back for your instruction." So people come in here all the time and they ask, "Do you give instruction?" No, but we'll help you fig-ure it out. The old way kept people very dependent by not giving them the gestalt of what they were doing. They would knit ten inches and come back, and then the old lady would do the decreases and say, "OK, now knit another ten rows and come back in a week." It was piecemeal;

you had no control, no power, no input. I never asked for instruction; I'd make my own things, little funky things, like scarves.

Every few years I'll just make something if I feel like it. The last time around, I went to knit and I made that sweater up there. [She points to a piece folded high up on a shelf.] Someone I know had a baby, so I just decided to knit it a sweater. I went to a yarn store uptown—far away. It was a very unsatisfying experience; I didn't feel comfortable, because to me, knitting has a lot to do with community, but I'm not sure exactly how. I left there thinking, *I need to open a yarn store in my community.* I know how to run a businesses, because I was a florist for seventeen years, and I had sold that store, and I was kind of thinking about my next move. I saw this store for rent and it became clear.

It was the way yarn was displayed in other shops that was the most disturbing thing to me. Nobody considered it. I thought, *This yarn is beautiful,* so I wanted to show it as beautiful. I have a system with the yarn— it's not to be articulated. People seem to like the left side of the shop better; it's the cheaper yarn, so it's a little gaudier. I keep the bulkier yarn away from the door, because I think people were stealing it. But arranging the yarn is the fun part. And then there's the part in my heart, the part about community. I live right upstairs, and I love that my neighbors come in and hang out. I think it's a positive thing for this neighborhood. We're just about to start knitting things for babies, for the United Nations to send to places like Afghanistan. Once a week or once a month, we'll sit and we'll each make a square and sew them together. From every sitting, we'll have a blanket to donate. After September 11, people were so anxious to connect, and this is a really good place to do that.

LANA LE: With knitting, you can be brainless and yet productive. When I started early in 2001, I got inspired by the Brooklyn Handknit stuff at the shop in Williamsburg [see page 12]. I thought, *I could make this stuff.* I took a class, and I was really hooked. I had to do it every night, and I would wake up wanting to knit, but I'd have to go to work.

RITA: We never get to knit here. I knit a tiny bit two days ago—it's so rare.

LANA: When I discovered Rita's store, I would get inspired by the yarns: "I can make *this,* and I can make *this.*"

RITA: Today I feel like I can't wait to go home. I have something blocked, and it'll be dry—a little sweater.

LANA: I took a special project class here, and I really just clicked with Rita. I have a lot of respect for her; she's one of those people who just does it, figures it out. She works hard, and she's friendly and warm. I felt that way about the store, like it was like a small-town store. I said, "I wanna work for you."

RITA: And then Christmas came, and I was like, "Help!" My marketing strategy is trying to create a space that doesn't feel like the middle of Manhattan. My flower store was like that. It had a fireplace and a back-yard. The screen door on this shop has something to do with that.

LANA: It feels warmer to me; other yarn stores feel like an office . . .

RITA: . . . like a business. I sort of knew that we needed a yarn store in this neighborhood. I think I would have been surprised if people didn't want it. My daughter was starting to knit, and I saw that something was happening with knitting. Now I have no perspective on it; now it feels like there's no other world but knitting. I'm just on this block, upstairs or downstairs, then I go to my house in the country, where there's no one around. I have no perspective on what's going on in the rest of the world; I assume everybody's knitting.

LANA: I haven't been knitting that long, so I felt like a beginner when I first started working here. But because so many people are getting into it and there are so many beginners, I could help people; I knew more than they did, because they were totally new.

RITA: It's about paying attention, levels of concentration.

LANA: I've worked in retail before, and when you work in a clothing store, people just come in and don't expect anything of you. But since this is a knitting store, they look to you for advice, what your opinion is, and for your help. It's neat that you can help people.

RITA: I've always taught people: ceramics, arts and crafts, and to autistic kids; I'd never taught knitting before, except to friends. I love to teach people how to do things. I'm a potter; I'm a florist. It's part of who

I am. I had this group from Parson's come in, a textile-design class, and I gave them a knitting lesson. The teacher passed by and said, "I'd like to bring my students here for a lesson about yarn and some knitting." They came one morning—it was really fun. Lana, do you remember that woman who's boyfriend bought her that wonderful valentine? She has this idea that she wants to teach a group of kids from Harlem. They saw her knitting and they were like, "What are you doing? Can you show me?" She saw this little girl, Maya, who comes and works here, she's nine and a half years old. She comes once a week, and she knits and helps, and she's very competent. Nina saw Maya knitting here one day, and she thought it would be great for these kids if Maya could be her co-teacher. They'll just come here in small groups, and Maya and Nina will teach them to knit. I'll put my two cents in, I guess, about whatever comes up.

LANA: I have an aunt who tried to teach me to knit once, when I was ten, but she lived in another state, so I didn't have access to anyone if I had questions or made a mistake. What I think made me so hooked on it in the beginning was that I'm already a graphic designer, and a lot of times I have to put so much thought into a project. I liked that with knitting, I didn't have to think about it so much. I could see the progression. I like doing it at night, because after my long day of trying to figure everything out and using my brain, I can still be creative. Knitting is forgiving; it's OK if it's not perfect.

RITA: Not for you! I can't believe you're saying that; you're such a perfectionist.

LANA: She teases me all the time about it.

RITA: I'm a gardener. I think it's very common that knitters are also gardeners and cooks. I'm not sure what the connection is, but I know there's a huge one. I think flowers and yarn are related, something about color and texture and nature. At one point, I had this job—it was a big flower job, and I was using a lot of freelance florists, and we were making a million arrangements. We were talking, and one thing that came up was that all florists seem to be really good cooks, too. I think it goes for knitting; it's a continuum, a spectrum. It's all part of the same thing. It's such a feminine activity.

My son-in-law wanted to knit a present for his mother last Christmas, so he asked, "Will you teach me?" He knitted a beautiful scarf and never knit again. He's done that with sewing as well. They moved into an apartment, and he said he wanted to make the curtains. So I showed him—he was so good at it, awesome. Made the curtains perfectly, never sewed again. He's an economist, but he just likes to taste things. I've tried to get my husband to want to knit. Years and years ago, when we lived in Mexico, he wove, but he just doesn't want to know how to knit. He wants me to make things for him and then reject them. I have this tie, which I think is so nice. He criticized it one too many times, so I have it down here now. I'm pretty proud of it, actually.

LANA: He's worn that tie! I've seen him wear that.

RITA: He says there's something wrong with the way it knots.

ROB*: It is a little thick here; I don't know if it makes a difference going around. I see—the middle part of it is thin and then thick, and when you go to knot it, it doesn't make much of a knot. Maybe that's it.

RITA: There's this hat that I felted, and even then he said it was too big. I want to be able to knit to just practice stitches and learn techniques, but I don't do it enough. I feel as though I'm under pressure to make things for the store.

LANA: In the beginning, I was more like a sponge; I wanted to learn *anything*. I saw one of those knitting pattern books, and I wanted to make the patterns to see if they would work out—I did all these swatches. Now that I know a little bit more, I'm like, "I'm going to make this, and I'm going to make that." So I started to learn how to crochet, because I want to know how to make everything.

RITA: Knitting is a reflection. If you look at people's stitches, you can tell something about them. But isn't that true of everything? We are what we do. We're all knitting as we are, in our own way. I notice with myself, I made this top, and for some reason the back came out so much bigger than the front. It was looser in the back, and then in the front I tightened up. There was at least an inch difference. Some people are consistent; some people are erratic. Some people knit tightly, some people

*That's Rob, my husband, who accompanied me on many interviews all through California and New York City and upstate New York, who was a solace, a co-interviewer, a tireless companion and uncomplaining chauffeur. On this evening, arriving to meet me at Rita's shop toward the end of our interview, he was a good-natured tryer-on of garments rejected by Rita's husband, but mostly he was just hungry for dinner.

knit loosely. I tend to do both. Sometimes I like tight knitting. The teachers always try to tell you to knit loosely—that's their mantra. I do kind of like it better tight. But I learned, too, recently, that when you block something, it gets tighter. That's why I want to run upstairs. I'm interested to see how my little sweater came out.

LANA: When I got really obsessed with knitting that first year, I said, "I'm going to give knitted presents to all my family," about ten people. I started at the beginning of the year, making mostly scarves and hats. The first few months, they were wide, and then they started to get narrower. I tried different things; the last thing I made was for my father-in-law and by far that was the most complicated pattern and the most interesting— it was a Banana Leaf pattern. It had some twisted cabling, with this leaf all the way down. I made a couple things for my husband. I got him involved, made him come and pick out the colors he wanted.

RITA: There's something in a book about how every time you knit something for a man, it's a hex; he'll leave.

ROB: What are you saying by knitting for your husband?

RITA: I'm saying, "He might be happier buying his ties." I'll knit other things for him, but I'll wait till he asks, "Why aren't you knitting anything for me?"

Epilogue

Two things happened to change my whole outlook on knitting. The first came on gradually, creeping over my consciousness like a low fog, and that was boredom. Boredom with knitting books, boredom with the minutiae of instructions, boredom with the look of little squares, boredom with their clutter—in short, boredom with every aspect of the act of knitting swatches, despite a few happy successes. Sometime at the end of August, I vowed never to knit another.

The second occurrence was rather more sudden. I had come home from my trip to California to three very new people; and although there is nothing especially sudden about the idea of babies, if you have watched their mothers expand and worry and accumulate all manner of preparatory gear for several months, the actual arrival of babies happens oh-so-abruptly. First there is nothing (very loosely speaking, of course), only your friend with a serious *idea* mushrooming in her belly; then there is a whole other *someone*. Or, in the case of my particular circle of friends, three other someones. Yes, I was expecting these babies, but when they finally (suddenly) appeared, the significance of their ... *them-ness* rendered me absolutely agog. I was so grateful—for the fact of the babies as much as for their apparent completeness and the absence of lasting damage to their mothers—that I was seized with a desire to give them something, something that might manage to convey even one small particle of that gratitude. The only way I knew of to do that was to make something. The only way to make something that seemed at all appropriate was with knitting.

What kind of knitting, though? That was the looming question. I'd flitted in and out of knitting shops all summer long and picked up and played with all manner of knitted baby everything: little hats, tiny booties, jumpers, sweaters, mittens, toys. I fell in love with a pair of pink rabbit slippers and a hood covered with pompoms. But I still had no desire to trust myself in factoring the critical measurements of such garments, even on a miniature scale. And more than that, it occurred to me as, just for a hypothetical exercise, I ran through the execution of these garments in my head that I had even less desire to make something of someone else's design.

I started sketching out blankets, the only things I felt fully confident in tackling. I'd taught myself plenty of stitches, though, so I didn't see any reason these blankets had to be utterly simple: plain old garter stitch or a few colored stripes. Besides, I knew enough to know that simple blankets were definitely not my style.

The first sketch, for Emmett: a rich Prussian blue blanket, with bobbles peppering its surface and an all-around scalloped edge in lighter blue—maybe I'd even try my hand at crocheting again, just for that edging.

For Zoe: a cream-colored blanket in Moss Bordered Diamond stitch, with her name spelled out in Moss Stitch bumps down the right-hand side and a border made of long, looped Faggoted Fringe.

And for Olivia: a spring-green blanket featuring a panel with a tree design at its center, surrounded by a thick border of Seed Stitch, with a picot edging or a turreted one.

In the end, though, after all my deliberating about what to knit, the first thing I made was not a baby blanket, but a scarf. I half roll my eyes in amusement to think about it now; after my initial stubborn insistence that I would never, *never* . . . there it is, folded neatly in thirds on my living room table, waiting for a washing in Ivory soap and a wrapping of colored tissue so that I can present it on Sunday at a friend's fortieth birthday party.

The truth is, I was content to make this scarf. I ambled down to The Yarn Tree one afternoon and picked out colors—a light, slate blue (my friend's favorite) and a berry red—from three over-full shelves of Mountain Mohair, chattering with Linda all the while about upcoming events at the shop, and how my book was progressing, and the easiest way to knit onto an already-existing piece of fabric. I'd once enjoyed rolling skeins into balls, but I am an inherently impatient person and I quickly lost the taste for it; so I let Linda hand-crank the skeins into fore-shortened tubes for me on her wooden winder while we talked about all the funny and bizarre requests she'd had from customers in her first year of business. I'd already conceived of a vague pattern for my scarf, and I mapped it out for Linda. She let out an enthusiastic exclamation, and I promised to bring the completed scarf back to show her. Then I went home and started knitting.

My idea for the scarf changed even before I began. I decided to rib it instead of my first idea of knitting it in garter stitch, and I decided to use a particular selvage—a knit stitch at the beginning and end of each row, which I learned about in Catherine Lowe's journal—to keep it from curling. I started in blue, knit in a few stripes in red; when I'd decided I was a third of the way through, I made a line of blue bobbles down the center of the scarf, then finished with a few more alternating red stripes. The scarf was lacking a bit in oomph, so I decided to edge it in red. Then, less than thrilled with the prospect of the usual, braided-looking cast-off, I rummaged around in Elizabeth Zimmerman until I found a sewn one: The end of the yarn is threaded through a needle, drawn through the first two stitches, and back through the first, which is then slipped off.

The end result: a happy, quirky-looking length of stitches that makes me smile to see it, hold it, wrap it around my neck, and think about giving it away, and the knowledge that possibly anything, even a theoretically humdrum scarf, can give me pleasure if I knit it. Now I still have all my blanket patterns to work on. In the words of Susan Haviland, I better get busy.

[T]he longest lives are short; our work lasts longer.
—Rose Wilder Lane, Woman's Day Book of American Needlework, 1963

Bibliography

Bashō, Matsuo, Nobuyuki Yuasa, trans. *The Narrow Road to the Deep North and Other Travel Sketches*. Harmondsworth: Penguin Books, 1966.

Bonesteel, Michael. *Henry Darger: Art and Selected Writings*. New York: Rizzoli, 2000.

Conze, Edward, compiler and trans. *Buddhist Scripture*. New York: Penguin Books, 1959.

Eyre, Jane. *Needles and Brushes and How to Use Them: A Manual of Fancy Work*. Chicago and New York: Belford, Clarke & Co., 1887.

Fassett, Kaffe. *Glorious Knits*. New York: Random House Value Publishing, 1985.

Fougner, Dave. *The Manly Art of Knitting*. Santa Rosa, CA: Threshold, 1972.

Fryer, Jane Eayre. *The Mary Frances Knitting and Crochet Book or Adventures Among the Knitting People*. Philadelphia: The John C. Winston Co., 1918.

Giles, Lionel. *The Sayings of Lao Tzu*. London: John Murray, 1959 (1905).

Hartley, Florence. *The Ladies Hand Book of Fancy and Ornamental Work—Civil War Era*. Mendocino, CA: R. L. Shep, 1991 (1859).

Heron, Addie E. *Dainty Work for Pleasure and Profit*. Chicago: Danks & Co., 1891.

Homer, Richard Lattimore, trans. *The Odyssey*. New York: HarperCollins, 1991 (1967).

Hope, Mrs. *The Knitter's Casket*. I. Hope, Ramsgate, 1898.

Klein, Anne Carolyn. *Meeting the Great Bliss Queen*. Boston: Beacon Press, 1995.

Knitting and Crochet, Aldine handy series; no. 1. London: The Aldine Publishing Company, 1915.

Lane, Rose Wilder. *Woman's Day Book of American Needlework*. New York: Simon & Schuster, 1963.

Mascaró, Juan, trans. *The Dhammapada*. New York: Penguin Books, 1973.

———. *The Upanishads*. New York: Penguin Books, 1965.

The Modern Priscilla magazine. 1917–18.

Norbury, James. *Knitting is an Adventure*. London: Hurst & Blackett, 1958.

Pullman, Mrs. *The Lady's Manual of Fancy Work*. New York: Dick & Fitzgerald, 1859.

Reps, Paul, compiler. *Zen Flesh, Zen Bones*. New York: Anchor Books, 1989 (1961).

The Self-Instructor in Silk Knitting, Crocheting and Embroidery. New York: Belding Bros. & Co., 1884.

Sibbald, Mrs. M. & Helen Greig Souter. *Dainty Work for Busy Fingers*. London: S. W. Partridge. & Co.,1915.

Stevenson, Isabelle. *The Big Book of Knitting*. New York: The Greystone Press, 1948.

Stryk, Lucien, ed. *World of the Buddha*. New York: Anchor Books, 1969 (1968).

Thomas, Mary. *Mary Thomas's Knitting Book*. Dover, NY: 1972 (1938).

Tillotson, Marjory. *The Complete Knitting Book*. London: Sir Isaac Pitman & Sons, 1933.

Trümpy, E. *Le Tricot*. Glarisse, Switzerland: 1923.

Walker, Barbara G. *Charted Knitting Designs*. New York: Charles Scribner's Sons, 1972.

———. *A Second Treasury of Knitting Patterns*. Schoolhouse Press, 1998 (1970).

———. *A Treasury of Knitting Patterns*. Schoolhouse Press, 1998 (1968).

Warren, Mrs. & Mrs. Pullan. *Treasures in Needlework*. London: Ward & Lock, 1855.

Whiting, Gertrude. *Old-Time Tools and Toys of Needlework*. New York: Dover Publications, 1971 (1928).

Zimmerman, Elizabeth. *Knitting Without Tears*. New York: Fireside, 1995 (1971).

Appendix:
Where to Find Some of the Knitters
and Yarn Companies Mentioned
in This Book

Linda LaBelle

www.theyarntree.com

Elizabeth Morse

www.uwc-usa.org

Clara Parkes

www.knittersreview.com

Susan Haviland

For teaching info:
sbhaviland@attglobal.net
For info on Lion Brand products:
www.lionbrand.com

Arlene Mintzer

For info on classes:
The Sensuous Fiber
P.O. Box 44 Parkville Station
Brooklyn, NY 11204
For digital images of the artist's work:
Julie Artisans': julie762@aol.com

Allison Dalton and Callie Janoff

www.churchofcraft.org

Hilda Erb

www.whatwouldbetseydo.com

Shannita Williams-Alleyne	www.craftydiva.blogspot.com
Vickie Howell	www.mamaramastyle.com groups.yahoo.com/group/stitchnbitch-austin
Edith Eig	www.laknitterieparisienne.com
Ellen Margulies	www.naturallycurly.blogspot.com
Mel Clarke	www.wildfiber.com
Suzan Mischer	www.knitcafe.com
Teva Durham	www.loop-d-loop.com
Trisha Malcolm	www.vogueknitting.com
Catherine Lowe	www.thecoutureknittingworkshop.com
Roxanne & Nyle Seabright	www.artfibers.com
Geri Valentine	To contact the artist directly: geri04606@yahoo.com For calendar info: www.wearingwool.com
Barbara Levin	www.TwistedSistersKnitting.com
Kathryn Alexander	www.kathrynalexander.net
Kirsten Hudson	www.getcrafty.com
Lana Le	www.woolypear.com
Rita Bobry	www.downtownyarns.com
Jamie Harmon Yarns	For a catalog and samples, send $4 to: 175 Barber Farm Road Jericho, VT 05465

Acknowledgments

This book, and my writing of it, would have been impossible without the input, generosity, and general goodwill of many, many people. I offer my profound gratitude to all the knitters who agreed to be interviewed for this project; they proved a patient, thoughtful, and supportive group who shared not only their stories but also, often, deeply personal pieces of themselves. They *are* this book—its heart and its voice—and I am so fortunate to have found them.

I am doubly indebted to Stéphane Houy-Towner at the Irene Lewisohn Costume Reference Library at the Metropolitan Museum and Elizabeth Browan at the Cooper-Hewitt library; to Linda LaBelle, the always-enthusiastic proprietress of my local neighborhood yarn shop, who went out of her way to cheerlead this project and whose kindness is legendary; to Kim Kauffman, pom-pom maker extraordinaire; to Rita Bobry of Downtown Yarn, who let me sit in her shop for hours and yack and yack and yack; to Clara Parkes of *Knitter's Review,* always at the ready with answers and encouragement; to Vickie Howell and Tina Marrin, my delightful West Coast pen pals; and to Erika deVries, who I think I can safely count, now, as a friend.

I extend very special thanks to Polly Segal, Sanjiv Bajaj and Kaumudi Marathé and Keya, and Janet Cowan and Mark Haber, who put me up (and put up with me) during the course of my California research. To Elanor Lynn, who lends spirit to this book and without whose astonishing expertise I would be lost. And finally, to my editor and friend Sara Carder, for making everything possible.

So You Want to Learn How to Knit?

1. Congratulations!

2. Look up knitting shops near you. Visit a couple and see if you like the atmosphere and, of course, the yarns. Ask if they host meetings or offer beginners' classes.

3. Go online. There are many knitting resources on the Internet, from how-to sites to blogs to magazines that do reviews, as well as listings of groups that have weekly or monthly meetings.

4. Check out knitting magazines such as *Vogue Knitting* and *Interweave Knits*. *Rebecca* is a German knitting magazine that is full of chic patterns.

5. Read Elizabeth Zimmermann's *Knitting Without Tears*, which is a classic. The *Family Circle Easy Knitting* magazines have very basic patterns.

Happy knitting!